CW00968513

Portuguese Tiles

from the National Museum of Azulejo, Lisbon

João Castel-Branco Pereira

Portuguese Tiles

from the National Museum of Azulejo, Lisbon

INSTITUTO PORTUGUÊS
DE MUSEUS

SCALA BOOKS

© 1995 Scala Books, London/
Instituto Português de Museus, Lisbon

First published in 1995 by Scala Books
143–149 Great Portland Street
London W1N 5FB

Reprinted 1998

Distributed in Canada and the USA by
Antique Collectors' Club Ltd
Market Street Industrial Park
Wappingers' Falls
NY 12590
USA

ISBN 0 302 00661 3

Scientific co-ordination: João Castel-Branco Pereira,
Director of the National Azulejo Museum

© 1995 Photos Instituto Português de Museus, Lisbon
Photography: Arquivo Nacional de Fotografia (National
Photographic Archives)
Photographic co-ordination: Vitória Mesquita, José Pessoa
Photographers: José Pessoa, Luis Piorro
Assisted by: Alexandra Pessoa, Sofia Torrado, Élia Marques
© Pedro Ferreira, José Rúbio, Francisco Matias, Manuel
Palma, Carlos Monteiro, Vitor Branco, Arnaldo Soares,
José Gomes Ferreira (No. 73, 102), Paulo Cintra,
Laura Castro Caldas (No. 140)
Collaboration: Emilia Tavares, Maria Alexandra Ribeiro

Editorial co-ordination: Isabel Cordeiro, Maria Amélia
Fernandes Instituto Português de Museus
Designed and typeset by Andrew Shoolbred
Translated from Portuguese by Peter F. Ingham
English translation edited by Moira Johnston
Produced by Scala Books, London
Printed and bound in Italy by Sfera/Garzanti, Milan

Contents

Acknowledgements

Fundação das Casas de Fronteira e Alorna

Instituto Português do Património Arquitectónico e Arqueológico

Metropolitano de Lisboa

Museu de Aveiro

Museu Nacional de Arte Antiga

Palácio Nacional de Queluz

Palácio Nacional da Vila, Sintra

Patriarcado de Lisboa

Tom Scoville

Note: The term *azulejo* which appears throughout the text is the Portuguese word for wall tiles and, in the present context, refers particularly to decorated tiles. The word probably derives from the Arab 'az-zulaca' – brilliant surface.

Measurements are given in centimetres, height before width. In the main section of plates where an inventory number on its own is given, the item belongs to the National Museum of Azulejo.

Foreword

The *azulejo*, together with carving, is the most widely used form of decoration in Portuguese national art. It is one of the few that can rightly take its place in a museum devoted to the greatest of all the Portuguese plastic arts.

Used continuously throughout Portugal's history over a period stretching back to the Middle Ages, the *azulejo* has now acquired renewed vigour, while reflecting the organic eclecticism of a culture that was both expansive and open to dialogue. It has embraced the lessons of Moorish artisans and was inspired by the ceramics of Seville and Valencia. It later adapted the ornamental formulae of the Italian Renaissance, while not ignoring the exoticism of oriental china, and, following an ephemeral period of Dutch inspiration, it created fantastic story-panels in blue and white that set the tone for a perfect assimilation of such varied elements.

Destiny was to turn the riverside convent of Madre de Deus into the National Museum of Azulejo, putting to good use a large collection of Dutch tiles that already existed in the body of the church. Since then the Museum has been a dynamic exhibition, taking full advantage not only of its collections but also of their evident quality and being transformed through concentrating on the modern plastic arts, into a landmark of Portuguese and European contemporary art.

This publication, which is the result of recent and propitious institutional collaboration, was an item missing in an otherwise well-organized museum. From now on, this work, which has brought together most opportunely the combined activities of expert research and publication, will be a symbol of this living, acting museum, a cornerstone of the strategy aimed at disseminating knowledge of Portuguese art.

Simonetta Luz Afonso
Director of the Instituto Português de Museus

THE CONVENT OF MADRE DE DEUS

THE BUILDING

1
The south façade portal. Uncovered
during 19th-century reconstruction work,
it was subject to considerable restoration.

In 1509, in the month of June, a small group of nuns who had recently arrived from the Convent of Jesus in Setúbal established themselves in the new convent of Nossa Senhora da Madre de Deus (Our Lady of the Mother of God). The following month the convent was blessed by the archbishop of Lisbon, Dom Martinho da Costa. The nuns, all of whom were discalced Franciscans of the first Order of St Clare, were indebted to Dona Leonor, Queen of Portugal, for the purchase of a few houses, complete with a vegetable garden, from the widow of Álvaro da Cunha, and for the construction of a modest nucleus of buildings that were to house them. The church, fundamental to the community, was only completed at a later date.

Royal sponsorship of similar foundations was common in those days. In this case, however, the munificence of the royal patron exceeded a mere matter of religious feelings. Dona Leonor (1458-1525), first daughter of the Dukes of Beja, was married young to Prince John, the future King João II. In a period of great political turbulence, the Queen saw her brother killed by her husband and witnessed the bloody finale of a conspiracy against the King himself. In 1491, a fall while riding killed the heir to the throne and João II, now without an heir, endeavoured unsuccessfully to legitimize his bastard son Dom Jorge of Lencastre. In 1495, following the monarch's death, Dom Manuel, brother to Dona Leonor, was acclaimed king. This heralded an age of unmatched splendour, marked by a continuous flow of exotic treasure from the Orient following the opening up of new maritime routes, the classification and growth of knowledge and a new manner of understanding the world.

The patronage of Dona Leonor clearly reflected the current perplexities. Still bounded by the mediaeval sense of universal interdependence, she founded the brotherhood of Our Lady of Mercy, a religious institution that responded to the increasing problem of urban begging with proverbial Christian *caritas*. Along the same lines, she founded Portugal's first large hospital at Caldas de Óbidos (1485), now known as Caldas da Rainha. In the same town she also sponsored the construction of a church that perfectly represented the more stimulating currents of

late-Gothic architecture, and the same traditionalist taste was apparent in her patronage of somewhat anachronistic regional painters. Open to the innovations of her time, Dona Leonor nevertheless also displayed a capacity to accept more progressive ideas. She provided support to artists' workshops in which the influence of proto-Renaissance models could be seen, such as that of the painter Jorge Afonso, Cristóvão de Figueiredo or the Master of Lourinhã. In Northern Europe, in Germany and in Flanders, she acquired a series of excellent panel paintings, one of which included herself in an attitude of prayer. The reliquary of gold and precious stones that she left to her Convent of Madre de Deus, probably made between 1510 and 1520, is one of the more remarkable pieces of Portuguese goldsmiths' work. Designed as a miniature architectural model, in the purest Renaissance style, it symbolically reproduces Celestial Jerusalem, just as described in a work printed in 1515 by order of the Queen.

The Convent of Madre de Deus was built in one of the pleasantest spots within the boundaries of Lisbon. Beside the river, in an area planted with vegetable gardens and orchards that supplied the city, it was also an old summer resort. It had been the site of a royal palace, which was already in ruins at the time of Afonso V, and in the 15th century one of Afonso de Albuquerque's grandmothers chose nearby Xabregas to found a Franciscan convent.

We know little today of the original nucleus of the convent (illustration 1). There is one (presumably reliable) picture in one of the panels of a retable showing the arrival of St Auta's relics and the removal of the martyr's mortals remains to Madre de Deus, an event that actually took place in 1517; this provides some precious information about the contemporary façade but suffers the want of precision in the drawing of the architecture which is apparent in the proportions of the buildings and in the exaggeration given to the decorative details. The convent consisted of four adjacent, staggered buildings, the annexe to the convent and the church, including the choir and the high altar. The façade of the church, the most outstanding feature of the whole, contains a skilfully designed portal consisting of ogee arches flanked by Salomonic columns,

2
Ground floor of the *Claustrim*, or Small Cloister. The 17th-century *azulejo* revetment came from the former Sant'Ana Convent, applied during the 1800s.

3
Upper floor or gallery of the *Claustrim*. The Romanticism that underlay the 19th-century restoration gave rise to some fantastical architectural compositions, seen in the arches.

2

3

4

4
The João III Cloister. Though documents show that the Renaissance architect Diogo de Torralva was linked to its construction, several late-Gothic traces suggest that the work was begun during the first half of the 16th century.

together with a medallion set on a bracket. There was a flourishing trade in such ceramic plaques from the Florentine workshop of the Della Robbia family, which spread throughout Europe cheaper copies of Italian Renaissance sculpture. Those that existed at Madre de Deus – consisting of six medallions and a tabernacle frontal, set on the façade and in the galleries of the main Cloister – mirrored the range of tastes of the monarchs, who were already aware of the new artistic ideas that contrasted with the general architectural styles leading up to the Manueline period. The probable platband finials of the original building, with their *fleur-de-lis* motifs, should also be mentioned: although as a motif they disappeared, they were later taken up again by the tendency towards reintegration that developed in the 1800s, one that was particularly interested in recovering the 'exotic' values of the building.

It is difficult to make out, from the present lay-out of the convent, what has survived from the buildings of Dona Leonor's time. In the church, besides the original layout, it is hard to detect traces of what existed before the rebuilding of the second half of the 16th century. The bell tower, with the exception of a few changes, may also date from the same period, several themes from the south façade recurring here. What is now the low choir, reached today from the Great Cloister to the church, and an adjacent room known as the Dom Manuel Room, are perhaps among the older surviving structures. The intimate atmosphere of the Small Cloister, also called the *Claustrim* (illustration 2), and of the 'Arab Room' recalls the time of the convent's foundation and is underlined by the singularity of the eleva-tions – although the gallery is a 19th-century addi-tion (illustration 3). The ground floor colonnade, consisting alternately of grouped three and two round arches under a single head on each side rest-ing on elegant columns with very simple capitals, pronounced abacuses and bases, the circular sections of which are decorated with palmettes, reveals the architectural and decorative simplicity characteriz-ing much of Portuguese late-Gothic architecture, a version of Mediterranean ideas deeply rooted in the spirituality of the late Middle Ages. A buckled cor-don encircling the perimeter of the Cloister – an example of the kind of naturalist decoration so evi-dent in Manueline architecture – constitutes the only light touch on this ground floor, a touch of per-sistent archaism in the middle of the reign of King Manuel I. The ceiling of the 'Arab Room' which opens on to the large Cloister is of *alfarge* – a mul-tiform Iberian decoration – with a noteworthy star design, a 16th-century reminder of the kind of work done by Moorish artisans and bearing witness to the prevailing taste for the exotic – even though it has been adulterated by 19th-century restoration.

The group of buildings left by Dona Leonor on her death was small. The nuns complained of this, although later they recalled with gratitude not only the origins of their first home but also the vast remodelling campaign carried out by João III. In more than one sense, the extensive reconstruction work carried out in the latter period marked a new

5

5
The sanctuary and dome over the cross-ing. The high altar was rebuilt after the 1755 earthquake. The image is of Our Lady of Contentment.

foundation of the riverside convent. The initial pre-text for royal intervention was to safeguard the building against the tides that regularly troubled the nuns and shook the foundations of the convent. Alterations to the river bank along this part of the Tagus and the construction of protective measures have been documented since 1523, although the plan to build a quay there was recorded in an order issued by King Sebastião I in 1567. In addition to the obvious commercial use for the wharves which were concentrated in eastern Lisbon, they also served as a base for the royal family and the aris-tocracy to enjoy recreation on the river, certainly more frequently after the convent was built and the royal palace at Xabregas enlarged.

The safety of the complex having been assured, João III was at last able to transform the convent. In the main, the reconstruction of the Madre de Deus Convent was part of the cultural renewal of the reign of João III. This policy of renewal represented a break with the past and approached the models of humanism and classicism, taken directly from Italy by the numerous Portuguese artists who went there, at the royal treasury's expense, to seek remnants of Antiquity and contact with the flourishing intellec-tual environment. The extent of the royal involve-ment right from the outset is suggested by the selection of Diogo de Torralva (c. 1500-66) to head the work. He was closely linked to the great build-ing of the Jerónimos Monastery, Belém, where, in 1551, he was the 'Master of Works'. He was also known for his military engineering projects and took part in the fortification of the port of Mazagão in Morocco. Torralva's greatest work, however, was the magnificent cloister of the Convent of Christ in Tomar, begun in 1557, a masterpiece that revealed his knowledge of Italian architecture and the mod-els set out by Sebastiano Serlio and Andrea Palladio.

Diogo de Torralva's links with the Madre de Deus Convent were documented from 1551 and almost certainly lasted to the end of the decade. The work, which added considerably to the comfort of the community, was focused on restoring the church and building the new Cloister (illustration 4). The aim was to improve the articulation of the latter and to create a sense of monumentality in so enclosed a

space. The structure of the Cloister is clear, with five arches to each elevation, the rhythm being set by the powerful buttresses. While the ground floor is provided with round arches, the upper floor has a gallery with architraves resting on slender columns, an unusual arrangement in Portuguese Renaissance architecture. Diogo de Torralva's control over the work was not continuous, or attentive; there can be no other explanation for the late-Gothic details in several of the columns of both floors and for the much poorer composition than that of his other work, such as the cloister at Tomar. The church was probably entirely rebuilt during the reign of João III, although, as we have seen, its layout was unchanged. The old portal was bricked up, although entry continued to be from the side, as was required for a nunnery: in its place there was built a con-temporary portal with two side columns and an architrave, over which there is a triangular pedi-ment.

The Madre de Deus Convent escaped from the 17th century almost untouched, with the exception of the minor maintenance work required by a build-ing of this size. The fabulous riches of Brazil and the spirit of the magnificent reign of João V reached the convent at the same time as many other of Lisbon's churches, filling them with gilded carving and *azulejos*, polychrome marbles and sacred furniture made of rare woods provided by the Conquests. The Sacristy was altered in 1746, the work of master-car-penter António da Silva and master-carver Félix Adaúto da Cunha. The work involved the doors, great chests and the carving of their lids and the frames of paintings by André Gonçalves. During the 18th century a dome was built over the crossing and the church's interior was further enriched by carv-ing and tiles. Following the great earthquake of 1755, a rococo retable, provided with the very large throne, was added to the Sanctuary (illustration 5).

The extinction of the religious Orders in 1834 and the sales of national property changed the his-tory of the convent. In 1871 a team co-ordinated by the learned architect José Maria Nepumoceno pre-sented a project for the conversion of the conventual buildings into the 'Dom Maria Pia Asylum'. The plan included a small museum. The work, begun by

Nepumoceno and continued by Liberato Telles, altered the whole of the conventual part, adapting it to its new role. In the grander areas, however, the aim was to recover the supposed original designs. The historicist attitude of the architects and those in charge of the work is understandable within the late-Romantic culture. This demanded an overall unity – eliminating discontinuities, imposing sequential rhythms to the fenestration – but also a return to the original essence of the building, as though it had not been burdened with alterations, inevitable over its four centuries of history. According to the records, the south portal was reopened or, presumably, rebuilt in accordance with the St Auta panels. Openings were made in the façade and provided with Manueline framing, while a heavily worked platband and fantastic gargoyles of a mediaeval nature were added. The most curious detail of

these alterations reveals, however, limits to the empirical archaeology of the 19th-century builders: on one of the capitals of the columns on the gallery of the Small Cloister is the carved image of a steam engine; perhaps the carver was divided between his fascination for technical matters and speed, and the sense of suspension of time that is evoked by the place.

Well into the 20th century, the architecture of the convent once again suffered alterations, particularly during the 1950s, in 1983 and in 1994. These were minor changes to adapt the building to the new requirements of the Museum, although they maintained and enhanced the general direction that had been established during the past history of the convent.

Miguel Soromenho

THE INTERIORS

'Her Serene Highness, Queen Leonor, wife to King João II, desirous of founding a Convent of Retired Nuns … The beginning of the foundation of the Convent took place in the year 1509 … And thus she chose from the Convent de Jesus Mother Colleta to be Abbess & another six Nuns, all of a great spirit; who took possession of the said new House …' (Santa Maria, 1707 pp. 124–5).

Queen Leonor was to profess in this House, although with no votive obligations. This allowed her not to comply with the requirement for seclusion, although until her death in 1525 she did live a community life at the Xabregas Palace next to the convent, outside the city walls at Lisbon's eastern gate. The history of the convent – its location, its ambience, its objects of worship and devotion – has always been linked to miracles and myths, which undoubtedly contributed to the enormous numbers of the faithful who came here. Little remains of the original building, but the magnificent patrimony left by the foundress bears witness to the commitment and devotion of the Queen and to her important role as a patroness and protector of the arts and thinking in Portugal. She stimulated and subsidized the publication of several important works, such as *Vita Christi*, *Boosco Deleytoso*, *Espelho de Crisitina* and the dramas of Gil Vicente. Tradition has it that the *Auto da Sibila Cassandra* by Gil Vicente was played for the first time at the convent. She ordered works of art from Flanders and Italy and from Portuguese workshops to decorate the building which she founded. These reflect a profound knowledge of the art of her times.

Almost all the treasures were removed to the National Museum of Ancient Art (Museu Nacional de Arte Antiga) at the beginning of the 20th century. An exhaustive inventory here would therefore be out of place, although they should nevertheless not be forgotten, for they represent a true expression of the Queen's artistic understanding and of the riches of the convent. The most important of the many works include the St Auta retable from the 16th-century Portuguese school; a reliquary of gold, enamel and precious stones, containing a thorn from Christ's crown, an object of great devotion that

6
St Anthony Chapel. 18th-century decorative assemblage; walls lined with *azulejo* panels and paintings alluding to St Anthony of Lisbon.

belonged to the royal treasury of King Duarte, which Queen Leonor donated for public veneration, now considered as a masterpiece of goldsmiths' work; the Madre de Deus retable from the workshop of Jorge Afonso, 1515; the Nossa Senhora das Dores polyptych, from the workshop of Quentin de Metsys, between 1504 and 1511; and the medallions (illustration 7) from the Della Robbia workshop, 16th century.

Having become the patroness of the convent, Dona Leonor conferred royal protection on it, a status it lost only on the extinction of religious Orders in Portugal in 1834. It was kept even during the period of domination by the Spanish monarchy, as can be seen from the donation by Empress Maria, sister of Philip II of Spain, of a piece of the Holy Cross.

Despite strict precepts of humility, penitence and particularly severe poverty governing this Order, observed in a most exemplary manner by the Xabregas nuns according to reports at various times, the convent was enriched and enlarged on various occasions. This involved the receipt of relics and valuable works of art, graces and privileges, enlargements and alterations, particularly during the reigns of João III, João V and José I. The Church, and in this case the mendicant Orders, did not value the works of art as material riches, but as an expression of beauty – an exaltation of God – and so the treasures of the convent do not contravene that most important of Franciscan rules, poverty.

Although subject to repairs, restoration and on many occasions adaptation to a new spirit from the middle of the 16th century, the buildings adhered to the layout required by a convent: church, choir, chapter house and cloister, the result of the work carried out during the reign of João III. In contrast, it is through the internal alterations that the artistic and dynamic evolution of official taste as an expression of royal will can be traced. Many contemporary documents bear witness to the royal involvement, principally the decorative work to the whole building during the reign of João V. The convent is therefore an important source of evidence in the history of art in Portugal, one example of the Port-

uguese baroque movement in its decorative programme created during the 18th century, which renewed its interiors.

In the church, which is structurally simple, the decoration, which is rich both in its forms and in the materials employed, achieves, through combination and harmony, an exuberant visual effect (illustration 5). This solution to the provision of unity through the *azulejos* and the carving – employing the same repertory of ornamental and pictorial representation which whatever their support (canvas, panels, *azulejos* etc.), has engraving as its source – has been an inspiration for the interiors of many buildings, particularly religious ones. One of the principal aims in creating the church has thus been achieved, that of persuading the viewer. The decoration of the convent was undertaken not merely for aesthetic reasons; the artistic quality of the works was usually subordinate to a programme essentially aimed at reviving faith. Art was a means to devotion; it should teach and move the faithful, while at the same time transmitting the ostentation of the monarchy and the drama of dogma, all expressions of the society of the times.

The absence today of several works in this building, or alterations to others, does not prevent an understanding of its iconographic programme, which was in keeping with its intentions to promote the doctrine of devotion to the Virgin, the transmission of the narratives of the Gospels and the moralizing exemplars of the lives and martyrdoms of the saints and was in accord with the spirit of the building and of its religious Order. The church, designed as God's palace, has three nuclei – the nave, the crossing and the sanctuary. These define the areas of the liturgical programme, expressed through art, and correspond to the spaces reserved for each level of worship, establishing a hierarchy in which the nave is reserved to the faithful and the sanctuary, on a higher level, to the clergy.

A complex programme of devotion to and exaltation of Mary, the Mother of Christ, proclaimed Mother of God since the Council of Ephesus (431), was carried out in this church, which was particularly devoted to her. Indeed, the Virgin has always had reserved to her a very special place in Christian

7

St Matthew. Medallion from the Della Robbia workshop. Italy, early 16th century.

8

Church, side wall with 18th-century *azulejo* revetment and painting, with carved frames. Side altar, 18th-century, with the relics of St Auta, given by Emperor Maximilian to Queen Leonor.

8

history, and many churches are dedicated to her. The Counter-Reformation strengthened her as a symbol of victory over heresies. The religious Orders were charged with exalting the new religiosity, and the Franciscans, with their apostolic ideal, played a fundamental role in disseminating Marian culture.

The *azulejos* lining the lower parts of the nave walls include a panel of *Moses and the Burning Bush* by the Dutch painter William van der Kloet, *c.* 1698, originally on the wall separating the church from the Low Choir and moved at the time of the alterations made by Nepomuceno. The theme, in a message of concord between the Old and New Testaments, is a prophecy, as is the bush that burns without being consumed, of the Virgin who was to conceive and give birth without sin. The introduction into Portugal of the cult of the Immaculate Conception, of Mary who by the will of God was conceived without sin, was the work of the Franciscans. The other tile-panels (illustration 8), representing hermits and scenes of Franciscan life, are a reminder of the intention of this space — to provide seclusion and silence — and were probably laid in the middle of the 18th century, when the pulpit was made. Along the lower parts of the walls is imagery representing the five senses (by the royal tribune) and the four elements of nature, which suggest that Man, in his various ages (symbolized by the natural elements), can through his senses rise up to God if he follows Christ's example. There are also two panels that date from the end of the 19th century by Pereira Cão (1841-1921), reproducing the panels of the St Auta retable that were used in the reconstruction of the convent's façade during the 19th century. Paintings and carvings fill the side walls at a higher level, structurally bounded by planes that are intrinsically linked to the hieratic artistic importance into which the arts were divided at the time — painting: major art; *azulejo*: minor art — with the carvings establishing a frontier.

Two paintings of devotional panels (see Glossary) narrate episodes in the lives of St Francis and St Clare in an extensive didactic programme seen as a unified whole and through their links. The two saints who founded this Order, in their role as guides, remind the faithful of the divine model.

9

9
Sacristy. Built *c.*1746-9, 18th-century decoration with great chests of exotic woods, the *Joseph of Egypt* cycle by André Gonçalves, and *azulejo* panels bearing the royal arms and the emblem of the Franciscans.

These paintings are an example of the militant art of this period, in which themes that had formerly been used in the service of the Faith still persisted but were now developed through a new energy, which found its expression in the narrative cycle. The St Francis cycle is placed in the first devotional panel, in direct contact with the faithful, like the Franciscans who brought the Gospels to the people. In the upper devotional panel, in contrast, the St Clare cycle, directly in contact with the choir – where the nuns said Mass every day and meditated – suggests female seclusion. These cycles are attributed to Bento Coelho da Silveira (1648-1708), with the exception of the painting flanking the triumphal arch, *St Clare* and *St Francis*, which are by André Gonçalves (1692-1762). Extension of the iconographic decoration to the ceilings, but limited almost to the *Life of the Virgin* or *The Passion*, reached its peak in the first half of the 18th century.

The Franciscan programme exalts Mary, Queen of the Angels, on the ceiling and on the triumphal arch, a tribute to the most venerated intercessor of saints and men. The triumphal arch, reserved for heavenly Marian themes (the Assumption, Glorification and Coronation), has a strong ideological meaning with its representation of the 'Crowning of the Virgin' set over the royal arms of Portugal. In this way, hierarchy and the message transcend the religious sense, in a demonstration of the direct emanation of the divine power of the King.

The combination of *azulejo* and gilded carving, both of which reflect light, provides an illusion of greater space. In addition to its role as a frame for the painting, the carving also highlights important architectural elements – entablatures, inner curves of arches, column shafts – and so reveals expressiveness and autonomy. The carving of the angles becomes almost sculptural, accenting the symbolism of the royal arms placed over the keystone. Of the side altars, one contains St Auta's relics – donated by Emperor Maximilian I, cousin of Queen Leonor – and the other depicts sculptures rather than paintings of the Holy Family. Despite the fact that they are not as splendid as other examples, they play their role of conveying illusion, and become canopies from which hang curtains of gold behind the centre of the composition. More exuberant in the modelling and forms are the various works carved by Félix Adaúto for Madre de Deus between 1747 and 1759. A fine example of this work is the pulpit, based on an engraving by Filippo Passarini, published in Rome in 1698 (Smith, 1968, p. 154).

The existence of a Tribune in the Sanctuary, the most sacred part of the church and therefore reserved for the higher levels in the hierarchy of the community, reflects the distinction accorded to the church by the royal family, and tradition has it that the kings often heard Mass here. The high altar (illustration 5) was rebuilt following the earthquake of 1755 in a different taste, seen in its almost graphic refinement and styling, which reveals a timid approach to the aesthetics of the late 1700s. The crowning of its pediment with sculptures of Faith and Hope emphasizes, through the absence of an image of Charity (the greatest of the three theo-

logical virtues) its spiritual presence as a fundamental tenet of the Church. The altar image is of Our Lady of Contentment, a large, polychromatic sculpture. It has a magnificent presence, heightened by the splendour of the surrounding gilt carving. This evocation of the Virgin represents the happiness of the Mother on seeing the Son of God resurrected and was the choice of the patroness of the church in order to bring a message of hope for the faithful.

The new Sacristy (illustration 9) was the result of the major reconstruction around 1746, under the aegis of Fr José Pacheco da Cunha, the head sacristan of the church, with the support of King João V. It has been entirely preserved, complete with its opulent decoration including: the ceiling painting of the *Assumption of the Virgin* (André Gonçalves); the Italian-style mosaic flooring; the round marble table for the placing of the vestments; the *azulejo* panel bearing the royal arms and the Franciscan emblems; and a great chest fashioned from exotic timbers, also the work of Félix Adauto da Cunha, the upper part of its front bearing three panels. These date from the 1500s, are by the Portuguese school and bear the images of St Agnes, St Luzia and St Catherine in harmony with the delicate carving work. This carving work is echoed in the frames of the paintings in the upper devotional panel, thus unifying the whole decoration of this room.

André Gonçalves worked for the convent from 1746 to 1750, painting eight panels depicting the *Life of Joseph in Egypt*. In 1759 he undertook the church's paintings already described above and retouched those of the Sacristy that had been damaged by the 1755 earthquake. Old Testament themes recur, foreshadowing the life of Christ, such as for example the scene of *Joseph Sold by his Brothers into Slavery*, symbolically used here as a prediction of the betrayal of Christ by Judas.

The Low Choir (illustration 10), within the Presbytery, is a part of the original building. Following the work carried out in the reign of João III in the middle of the 16th century, this became the Chapter House where formal gatherings were held, and it was also used as the convent's place of burial. At the end of the 19th century, this part was greatly altered: on the walls opposite the entrance to the church, a reliquary was placed to fill a void; the walls were decorated with ceramic tiles forming 'carpets' which, according to Liberato Telles, were '… the same as those that lined the walls of the gardens of the old convent, its corridors and refectories' (Telles, 1899, p. 18). The 16th-century Hispano-Moorish *azulejos* in the window bays were placed there because it was thought that this was their original position. The paintings, dating from the end of the 16th century to the 18th, and the Marian symbols painted on the ceiling, were inserted in empty frames rather haphazardly. The two 18th-century side altars of gilded carving are dedicated to Nossa Senhora da Boa Morte and to the Dead Christ. The theme of death, so representative of much of baroque art, is expressed in the complementary narratives of the Crucifixion and of the Ascension of the Virgin, who is presented here as the intercessor and guarantor of a serene passage, an image appropriate to a former burial ground.

The Cloister, attached to the church, was a fundamental axis of conventual life, used both to link the various areas and for the contemplation and meditation required by the community. In a cloister, a fountain symbolizes water pouring forth from Paradise next to the Tree of Life, which runs in the four cardinal directions represented here by paths bordered with flowers, shrubs and grass. The perpetual motion of the water represents, in the sacred conventual language, the certainty of eternal life ensured by the purification of baptism. In the centre of the Madre de Deus Cloister (illustration 4), built during the reign of João III, the Gothic-style fountain is unusual in that it is composed of six small atlantes supporting the basin. Borders decorated in Gothic script establish the following dialogues between the atlantes: 'Help me'; 'As best I can'; 'And you who help me not'; 'I can no more'; 'Very heavy'; and 'God help us'. The ceramic wall tiles that now cover the Cloister walls were put here at the end of the 19th century (see The History of the Collection). In the corners of the galleries are the devices of Leonor and João II: the pelican, a symbol of the sacrifice of Christ who died to redeem the sins of mankind, was adopted by the King together with the motto 'for the law and for the

people'; and the shrimp-net, which was the Queen's emblem in memory of Prince Afonso, whose body was covered on his death by a fishing net.

Close to the Low Choir, three tombstones remind visitors of Queen Leonor, her sister Isabel and the first abbess of the monastery, Sister Coletta. The so-called Leonor Room is here, the name perhaps given for its proximity to the tomb. The ceiling of this room is one of Portugal's few surviving examples of *mudéjar* influence (see Glossary).

In the small Cloister or *Claustrim* (illustration 2), which is still largely original, although with 19th-century wall panelling, is the St Auta Fountain, referred to over the centuries as a fount of miracles.

On the upper gallery of João III's Cloister the *azulejo* decoration shows *The Passion*, one of the principal themes for Franciscan devotions, transposing its steps to the 'Paths of the Cross', an obvious reminder of the vocation of the Franciscan Order, which was to be the guardian of the holy places. The power of the fundamental symbol of Christianity, the Cross, (re-)oriented by St Francis with a view to humanizing the Divine, is summarized in the words 'Take up your Cross and follow me'. St Teresa of Avila was to say of this image: '*En la cruz está la vida y el consuelo, y ella sola es el camiño para el Cielo*' - 'On the Cross is life and consolation, and only the Cross is the path to Heaven'. The representation of the 'Real Paths of the Cross' in this area allowed the nuns to make a spiritual pilgrimage accompanying Christ and meditating on his suffering.

This pilgrimage gave access to the Choir's antechamber, the devotional function of which was reflected in the images of saints and notable religious figures. During the second quarter of the 18th century, it came to be known as the St Anthony Chapel (illustration 6), for the evocation of this Franciscan saint, in a sermon that was an apologia for his life and work. This ornamental opulence that invaded the sacred areas of the convent with a mass of decoration that filled it completely − ceiling, walls and floor − creates an extraordinary and encompassing visual effect. The floor is made of exotic woods, and the walls are provided with eight tile panels dating from the first half of the 18th cen-

10

10
Low Choir. Former Chapter House; alterations were carried out during the 19th century, and its decoration was restored.

11
'Peasants', a group from the Madre de Deus *Nativity*, the work of António Ferreira, mid-18th century.

11

tury. These depict the more important of the hermits of hagiography, such as St Paul and St Anton. In the upper devotional panels of the side walls, a total of 27 canvases attributed to André Gonçalves relate the miracles, and the religious life of St Anthony of Lisbon is revealed on the ceiling.

The *Nativity*, a work attributed to António Ferreira, who was known as 'Ferreirinha de Chelas' (*c.* 1731-*c.* 1795), – and dating from the mid-18th century, was in the Casa do Presépiò (Nativity House), in an extension of this chapel, where it used to be put on display at Christmas. This work, for its modelling, for its exquisite draperies and chiefly for the expressiveness of the figures, is a very clear demonstration of the humanity that is so fully expressed in Portuguese baroque Nativity scenes (illustration 11).

The Choir, where the religious community heard and took part in the liturgy, forms part of the Sanctuary or Presbytery. In certain conventual houses, such as the female convents of seclusion, it was always separate, to a greater or lesser degree, from the outside world, giving rise to the so-called High Choir, which was located beyond the nave, at a higher level. Seclusion, which did not allow access to the body of the church, extended the function of the Choir, beyond the liturgical life of contemplation and meditation to which it is normally dedicated, to the celebration of conventual Mass through the presence of the Holy Sacrament in the Tabernacle. At Madre de Deus, the Choir (illustration 12) contributes to the spirit that, in the first half of the 1700s, presided over the transformation of the convent into a baroque building through decoration that here acquires a matchless monumentality. Use of the same materials – carving, *azulejo* and painting – created a marvellous space. All the elements come together in a harmonious combination that reveals great artistic quality and does not just give instruction in the Church's dogma but also consolidates its moral edification through spiritual stimulation. The iconographic programme established for the Choir, which does not have the didactic role of the church, was essentially designed to promote Christian morality. This was aimed at an assembly which understood the message of the scriptures and incessantly sought the path to saintliness, which could be achieved though an active, contemplative life and particularly a life of penitence.

In keeping with the wishes of its foundress, the convent never received alms. The nuns were obliged to provide for their own subsistence through work in the vegetable gardens and orchards, although hours of their daily life were spent in meditation, and their testimony speaks of the self-flagellation to which they submitted themselves. All this was complemented by the presence in the Choir of images intended to consolidate the mystic path to God. Unusually, this Choir was also used as the treasure house, a place to keep relics, the most precious objects of veneration; this increased its moral burden while also adding to its sumptuousness. The reliquaries that line the choir stalls are appropriately of carved gilt and they contain a magnificent set of relics, many of which were given by the monarchs, that made the convent famous.

The imposing Tabernacle (illustration 13) bears the symbols of power, again in a clear hierarchic structure in which expression of temporal power involves the royal shield surmounted by the Host, in turn surmounted by God the Father. The crowning, as in the high altar, carries figures of the theological virtues: Hope and Charity flanking Faith, the latter at a higher level. The structure and symmetry reflect a somewhat Italianate taste, close to being ephemeral architecture, with which it shares a sensuousness. The wood here was used not only as a vehicle for the splendid gilded carving but also for the flooring and for the antiphonal stands of the High Choir and the retrochoir. Witness to the other riches and taste present here, these treasures were made from the best exotic woods provided by the House of India (Casa da India), such as ebony, *lignum vitae* and *pau violeta*.

As in other areas, the paintings do not match the original programme and there are signs of substitution. An example of this is the *View of Jerusalem* (illustration 14), a panel of the Flemish school (1st half of the 16th century) in which, in addition to a portrait thought to be of Queen Leonor included after the panel had been painted, the entire iconography of the Passion of Christ can be seen. This panel, together with several of those that in the 16th century were part of the Madre de Deus retable, were still seen flanking the Tabernacle in 1940. Next to the altars are the portraits of *João III* (illustration 15) and *Queen Catarina* (illustration 16) with their guardian saints, which, according to Fr Jerónimo de Belém, were ordered by the monarchs themselves to be included. Attributed with being the second founders of the convent and portrayed in prayer, they found in this place a privileged spot for its proximity to the Tabernacle and left a permanent evocation of their memory among the nuns. The paintings, dating from the 16th century, now attributed to Cristóvão Lopes (1516?-70?) were modelled on the work of Anthonis Moro (António Moro), a painter at the Spanish court who was in Portugal around 1552. The other 17th- and 18th-century painting represented in this part by canvases decorating the ceilings and walls with themes from the *Life of the Virgin* and of *Christ* fulfils its role of decoration while helping to convey a spiritual message.

The windows, set at a very high level, strengthen

12

12
High Choir and treasure house. Temple of seclusion where the nuns met for worship.

the symbolism of the whole through the side panelling consisting of eight *azulejo* panels of the biblical heroines of the Old Testament in a way that symbolizes the Virgin's qualities. They reflect the sunlight, increasing the decorative and spiritual effect while at the same time conveying their intrinsic meaning through their position in this ensemble.

Teresa Campos
Alexandre Pais

13
Tabernacle. Magnificent 18th-century-
Italian-influenced carving.

14
View of Jerusalem
Oil on wood
Flemish workshop, *c.* 1510
Gift of Emperor Maximilian I to Dona
Leonor who donated it to Madre de
Deus

14

15
Portrait of *King João III*
Oil on wood
Portuguese school, attributed to
Cristóvão Lopes *c.*1564

16
Portrait of *Queen Catarina*
Oil on wood
Attributed to Cristóvão Lopes, *c.* 1564

15   16

THE HISTORY OF THE MUSEUM

17
Great View of Lisbon, detail with the
Madre de Deus Convent
Lisbon, *c.* 1700
Total measurements:111.5 x 2347
From the former palace of the Counts of
Tentúgal, Lisbon
Inv. 1

During the 1958 commemorations of the Vth centenary of the birth of Queen Leonor, an exhibition dedicated to her was held at the former convent of Madre de Deus, founded by the Queen in 1509. Nothing could be more fitting: the convent is one of the more eloquent testimonies to her work, a lifetime of patronage of the arts and of charitable works.

The exhibition involved much restoration work on parts of the convent, which had been altered on several occasions in a way that was not always sympathetic. The Directorate General of Buildings and National Monuments was in charge of the work and the recently created Calouste Gulbenkian Foundation made a substantial contribution of funds. The quantity of fine objects on display — many from the convent itself — and the design of the Museum by one of the great architects of the day, Francisco Conceição Silva, contributed to the success of the exhibition. This led to the creation of a museum in the newly refurbished convent solely dedicated to the *azulejo*. Indeed, the church and other areas of the convent were already provided with an extraordinary collection of ceramic panelling dating from the 17th and 18th centuries, both original work and tiles that were placed there during the late 19th century, when a great deal of restoration work was carried out. Since 1916 the National Museum of Ancient Art (Museu Nacional de Arte Antiga) had taken responsibility for the church and several of the other buildings considered as an annexe of the Museum and documenting the age of the Portuguese baroque. Allied to this was the dedication of the Museum's Assistant Curator in charge of the ceramic section, João Miguel dos Santos Simões (1907-72). He also headed the *Azulejo* Studies Brigade, set up by the Calouste Gulbenkian Foundation to make an inventory of the old *azulejos* that still existed in Portugal and in Brazil. A man of wide cultural interests, Santos Simões devoted most of his study to the *azulejo*, and in this field he acquired international renown and regard. The results of his research, published in articles and books, are a landmark in the study of this most important Portuguese ornamental art, and clearly reveal his exceptional qualities both as a researcher and as a historian.

17

On the other hand, what he did for the Museum also demonstrates his talent as a curator. Santos Simões was entrusted with the organization of the Azulejo Museum (Museu do Azulejo) in 1960, relying heavily, once again, on the support of the Calouste Gulbenkian Foundation. The Museum was finally opened to the public in 1965, when it was still considered to be an extension to Portugal's main museum. He was responsible for the temporary Azulejos Exhibition held in 1947, which brought together a collection that, kept to a great extent in reserve, '… was unknown to the majority of those who visit this house', as João Couto, the Director of the National Museum of Ancient Art, was to say in the catalogue. He continued '… on organizing the exhibition, the idea was not to gather together the best examples, such as those that line the churches and houses of Portugal … The idea was simply to show the evolution of this decorative art, providing examples of our *azulejos*, presented with certain educational criteria and, as far as possible, in chronological order.' This principle continues to govern the present exhibition. Indeed, since it was thought that large tile compositions should remain within the locations for which they were created, an exhibition of *azule-jos* as museum objects should constitute, as it were, an initiation in the study of the art, exemplifying its quantity, quality, variety and capacity to adapt to new tastes throughout five centuries of uninter-rupted use. The convent's panels undoubtedly pro-vide material for an appreciation of this aspect. The exhibition should stimulate the visitor to discover for himself a unique and original heritage scattered across the four corners of Portugal. For a better understanding of Santos Simões's concepts on research and the dissemination of knowledge, an unpublished document, dated 21 May 1970, entitled 'A description of the creation of an *Azulejo* Study Centre' is an excellent resumé.

The aims of the Centre, which is a part of the Museum although provided with its own facilities, included fostering studies of the Portuguese art of the *azulejo* in particular and of the use of ceramics in architecture in general; the publication of a bulletin providing information as to the work carried out; the dissemination of information and promotion of training courses with a view to stimulating the interest of the younger members of society in *azulejo* studies both in the field of historic and artistic research and in design; fostering relations internationally between specialists; creating a library and welcoming scholarship holders; and providing co-operation to private individuals, industry and educational institutions, etc. Current understanding of what the National Museum of Azulejo should be is not too different from Santos Simões's view of the combined Museum and Study Centre. Time and conditions have changed, but the principles set forth are still valid, and the Museum is itself a Centre for Ceramic Studies.

João Miguel dos Santos Simões was in charge of the Azulejo Museum up to 1972, the year of his death. He had not been able to enlarge the premises sufficiently to contain the vast store of pieces, consisting mainly of the collections of the National Museum of Ancient Art in addition to items received by the state as a result of its commitment to the collection of any *azulejos* that might otherwise have been lost when removed from buildings. Nor did his death allow him to complete the exhaustive inventory of 18th-century *azulejo* production in Portugal, published posthumously in 1979. However, his vast bibliography, the organization of an international congress on the art of the *azulejo* (Lisbon, 1971) and the creation of the Museum, gives him a place of importance in the context of Portuguese culture in the last half of the 20th century.

In the early 1980s, extensive building work was undertaken with a view to housing the nucleus of the XVII Exhibition of Art, Science and Culture, sponsored by the Council of Europe and devoted to the theme of 'The Portuguese Discoveries and Renaissance Europe' (1983). The work, designed by Prof. Sebastião Formosinho Sanchez, greatly enhanced the Museum and provided more space, although, for reasons of bureaucracy, the whole area of the former convent could not be used by the Museum. A second phase of activity was launched under the leadership of Rafael Salinas Calado, who had collaborated with Santos Simões and followed in his footsteps as the curator in charge of this section of the National Museum of Ancient Art.

18
Panel from a group depicting animals
hunting animals
c.1670

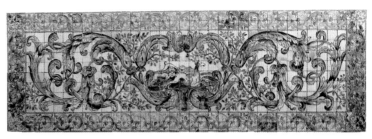

18

Calling attention to an art that is to such a large extent part of the day-to-day lives of the Portuguese and is understood as one of the more original manifestations of Portuguese culture, required administrative measures as well as the co-operation of the media. Decree-Law 404/80 of 26 September 1980 created the National Museum of Azulejo in 1980, and the curator in charge was appointed as its first director. At the same time, taking advantage of a temporary closure for building work, the director invested in an international travelling exhibition that was fairly representative of the art of the *azulejo* in Portugal. The exhibition was held at 24 different locations in 15 countries between 1979 and 1984.

Since 1987 a new management team has been formed. Its aim is to put into practice programmes that will turn the National Museum of Azulejo into an effective instrument with which to spread abroad information about this art, to provide for the advancement of knowledge in the subject within the discipline of the history of art, and to preserve and defend its status and quality in contemporary manufacture, in the conviction that the *azulejo* in Portugal cannot be allowed to become merely a matter of history. It should continue to attract both artists and designers and be able to rely on resources that will help it be accepted as an art suitable for public spaces. In order to spread abroad its activities and promote studies of this heritage, the Museum invests in organizing temporary exhibitions centred on almost-forgotten themes, research into which might constitute a real advance of knowledge. It also publishes the *Azulejo* journal once a year. In the field of conservation and restoration, technicians are trained so they are capable of preserving this heritage. Contributing to the conservation and to the study of ancient *azulejos* while also fostering contemporary manufacture is the ambition of the Museum, which is concerned too in disseminating knowledge of ceramics in general as well as of Portuguese *azulejos* and work from other countries, in a confrontation that can only be enriching. The Museum project, which has developed since 1989 and has been concerned with both the permanent display of items and the majority of the temporary exhibitions, relies on the collaboration of architect João Bento d'Almeida.

Several of the original functions of the convent are still maintained. The church, though an integral part of the Museum, is open for worship, and Mass is celebrated here, as are weddings and baptisms. The Museum spreads over all the other parts of the former convent, providing a range of environments and usage, some ancient and some contemporary, that preserves the spirit of one of the most sumptuous examples of Portuguese religious architecture.

João Castel-Branco Pereira

THE HISTORY OF THE COLLECTION

19
Eucharistic allegory
138.5 x 111
From the former Sant'Ana Convent, Lisbon
Inv. 161

The Exhibition of Ornamental Art held in 1882 at the Museum of Fine Arts (Museu de Belas Artes; now the National Museum of Ancient Art or Museu Nacional de Arte Antiga) was intended to provide the Portuguese with an opportunity to see a large number of objects belonging, in the main, to private collectors in addition to displaying several public collections. In some of the rooms there were a few exhibits of *azulejos*, such as some of those that the House of the Dukes of Braganza had ordered in Antwerp in 1558 for the ducal palace at Vila Viçosa, the small *Visitation* by Francisco Niculoso of the beginning of the 16th century, several Portuguese patterned tiles dating from the 16th and 17th centuries, and several 18th-century 'free-standing figures tiles'. (see Glossary).

There was no interest in the *azulejo* as a collector's item when, in 1914, an exhibition was organized at the former Carmo Convent, the nucleus of which was faience manufactured in the capital. Of the 265 catalogue entries only 22 dealt with *azulejos*, the greater part of which described just one tile. It would appear, therefore, that there were few collectors of *azulejos*, which were then being removed from a large number of buildings, especially religious buildings. The majority of the *azulejos* were to be installed in other buildings, not always in the best of taste. Secularization of the convents led the state to sell off many such buildings, which were then adapted to other purposes, although several continued under state ownership and in these cases such tiles as were removed were handed over to museums.

Thus it was that Santos Simões found a vast store of *azulejos* belonging to the National Museum of Ancient Art, the origins of many of which were not recorded.

The Madre de Deus Convent is one of the many examples where old tiles were re-used in different buildings. Many *azulejos* were added to those that had been expressly made for the convent – such as the Dutch panels by Jan van Oort, dating from about 1698, in the church (illustration 8); the large compositions dating from the second quarter of the 18th century in the St Anthony Chapel (illustration 6); or the panels dated about 1746-9 in the Sacristy

LOWADOSEIA
O SATISSIMO
SACRAMETO

19

20
Museum restaurant decorated with
19th-century *azulejos* from a kitchen in
Lisbon used for smoking hams

21

21
Main staircase with *azulejos*, 2nd quarter
of the 18th century, from the Calhariz
Palace, Lisbon

22

23

22
Alminha. Coimbra, 18th century, 2nd half
59 x 39.5
Acquired by the Museum in 1994, inv. 6177

23
Portrait of *Fernando Pessoa*, 1990
Project by Júlio Pomar (b. 1926), 1984
196 x 112
Donated by the Lisbon Metropolitano, 1990, inv. 1951

24
Lisbonne aux mille couleurs, 1992
Replica of the panel made for the Portuguese Pavilion at the Paris International Exhibition in 1937 (destroyed)
Project by Paulo Ferreira, 1936
224 x 224 cm
Donated by the Calouste Gulbenkian Foundation 1993, inv. 5928

24

(illustration 9). *Azulejos* brought here subsequently came from a variety of places, such as the convents of St Albert and Sant'Ana convents in the Grilós, and from the Calhariz Palace in Lisbon. The 72,905 *azulejos* that were brought to the convent at the end of the 19th century include the 17th-century chequered *azulejos* in the original Small Cloister (illustration 2); several 18th-century panels, such as the vases of flowers on the ground floor of the João III Renaissance cloister; the magnificent panels of *St Francis of Assisi* attributed to Manuel dos Santos in the so-called Dom Manuel room; the hunting scenes in the so-called 'cut-out' panels dating from the 2nd quarter of the 18th century which line the staircase (illustration 21); and the rococo compositions inspired by Van Haeften's engravings of the *Path of the Cross* on the first floor of the same classic cloister. Many others are still to be installed (illustration 19).

In recent years priority has been given to the acquisition of panels dating from before 1800 and of the vast output of patterned tiles used on façades of 19th- and early 20th-century residential buildings, in addition to the varied range of contemporary productions. The intention has been to fill in the gaps within the permanent exhibition so as to create a continuous record of tiles produced over the centuries.

Just three examples obtained through donations and purchases will give an idea of the way in which the collections were enriched.

In 1994 the Portuguese Museum Institute (Instituto Português de Museus) acquired from a private collector a very important set of 18th-century baroque, rococo and neo-classical *azulejo* panels (illustrations 22 and 97) representative of the output of Coimbra and Lisbon. These panels were originally part of the decoration of lay buildings and were of a style not previously found in the Museum's collection: of particular interest among these are four 'welcome figures' and several dated 'devotional panels' (illustrations 22, 61 and 96). Following the temporary exhibition in 1994, dedicated to Querubim Lapa, one of the most important Portuguese ceramicists of this century, Querubim offered a large number of pieces illustrating the various phases of his work, including *azulejo* panels, three-dimensional pieces and projects for wall ceramics. Lastly, the patronage of the Lisbon Underground (Metropolitano) should be acknowledged. Since 1990 the company has given replicas of the *azulejo* panels made to decorate all the underground stations and designed by Portugal's most famous artists (illustration 23). These gifts, in addition to those of other ceramicists, have provided a representative sample of contemporary design on a par with that of other ages in the collections of the National Azulejo Museum (illustrations 24, 141–149).

João Castel-Branco Pereira

THE COLLECTION

Azulejo panel. Seville, mid-16th century
54 x 40
Inv. 109

On visiting the palaces at Sintra, Fronteira or Queluz; on entering Coimbra Cathedral, the Misericórdia Church in Vila do Conde, the Marvila Church in Santarém or the Dominican Church in Elvas; in the cloisters of Oporto Cathedral or in Our Lady of Terço in Barcelos, in the Lóios Monastery in Évora or in the São Lourenço Church in Almansil; on taking the train at the stations of São Bento, Oporto or Beja or even on quickly passing through the Ribeira in Oporto next to the Dom Luís I Bridge or along the Infante Santo or Gulbenkian Avenues in Lisbon; on taking the Metropolitano in the capital; on strolling through the streets of Ovar or Caldas da Rainha – on visiting all these places even the most inattentive person will see that the ceramics on buildings and in spaces, both indoors and out, are extraordinarily diverse in their decoration and methods of application, even considering the four centuries through which these glazed, brilliant surfaces were manufactured. There are many thousands of examples. Indeed, the *azulejo* has been used continuously since the 15th century throughout the whole of Portugal and in such far distant places that were a part of her empire as Brazil. Its use is so widespread that it has become one of the more visible manifestations of Portuguese culture.

In 1845 the then Prussian ambassador in Lisbon, Count Athanasius Raczynski, wrote in his twenty-fourth letter to the Berlin Artistic and Scientific Society,

> The *azulejo* is a part of Portugal's physiognomy. *Azulejo* is the term they employ to describe the fine squares of kiln-fired clay, glazed on one side. Few churches or houses do not have them, They both frame doors to buildings and ornament vestibules and staircases. In the greater part of the houses, even in the poorer dwellings, the interior walls are lined with them to a height of three feet or more. There are houses that are covered with them from top to bottom …

Raczynski went on to say that the great historian Alexandre Herculano told him that 'in the early days of the Portuguese monarchy there was a need to employ Moorish architects and even workmen to build Christian churches' (fourteenth letter). Santos Simões admits the possibility that the many ceramic plaques made of homogeneous body, glazed with lead and coloured, some green, others honey-coloured, of various geometric shapes – crosses, stars, hexagons, squares and rectangles – that lined the floors of Leiria Castle were made by Moorish artisans who were already working in the area at the beginning of the 15th century. This type of paving formed 'carpets', in more or less complex forms, some of the elements of which are reproduced here in illustration 25. They are photographed from the back because centuries of use have worn them thin and many are almost completely eroded.

By the 13th century other ceramic revetments had been made in Portugal: the floor of the apse and its chapels at the great Cistercian abbey at Alcobaça, partly removed in 1939, was made of floor-tiles forming a 'carpet' of a simple geometrical design, using various colours – creams, browns and reddish tones – colours that reflected the shade of the clay covered with a colourless lead glaze or with glazing in which the lead had been mixed with pigments.

The roots of the ceramic decoration that was developed in Portugal must be sought not in Western Christian Europe but in the Iberian culture of the 15th century, in which the 'azulejo appears as a differentiated display, intimately linked to artisans of Moorish extraction' (Santos Simões, 1969). Whether directly imported or through the insinuation of taste, examples from the three great centres of Iberian ceramics at the end of the Middle Ages can be seen in Portuguese architecture: Valencia, Granada and Seville.

By the middle of the 15th century hexagonal plaques and small square tiles, called respectively *alfardons* and *losetas* (see Glossary), used for floor-lining in other central and western regions of Europe, had been imported from Manises (Valencia). These were decorated with *engobe*, coloured liquid clay. Generally speaking, tones of ochre with a clear lead glazing were preferred. But in the Spanish Levant (Paterna and Manises) the tiles, also with an *engobe* finish, were provided with two or three colours using, in addition to white lead, cobalt blue and the purplish brown of manganese. The composition formed by a *loseta* framed with similar hexagonal plaques (*alfardons)* produced a regular

octagon (illustration 26). Sometimes all the tiles were decorated; in other cases the central painted square was surrounded by brick *alfardons*. This explains why there are more *losetas* than *alfardons* still to be found in Portugal. The small Manises tiles at the Museum are decorated with motifs incorporating the human figure, animals, flowers or heraldry, the latter consisting of the coats-of-arms of the nobility or the emblems of corporations that, outside their country of origin, had no symbolic value. The decoration of the *alfardons* was mostly of stylized floral elements and motifs of sinuous lines recalling cursive Arabic script. In Portugal *losetas* and *alfardons* from Manises were employed in the flooring of the palace, extensively rebuilt in 1447, that the Dukes of Beja – the parents of the future king, Dom Manuel I – owned in the city of Beja. They were also employed in Lisbon at the Alcáçova royal palace and at the Casa dos Bicos, a noble residence built by Brás de Albuquerque in 1523. The tiles that were found here were probably from an earlier building that had existed on the site. *Rajolas*, another type of Manises square tile that was larger and made towards the end of the 15th century, were employed in the Royal Palace at Sintra and in the Quinta da Bacalhoa manor house, not far from Lisbon. They are still to be found at the convent of Jesus in Setúbal where the decoration of the *rajolas* in a stylized representation of straight ropes, linked together by knots, that cross over, create a white network on a blue background. These completely line the octagonal plan, stepped floor leading to the lavabo-fountain in the cloister. The Museum also houses identical tiles from the Alcáçova Palace (illustration 27).

The decoration of Manises tiles combines motifs common to European Gothic with the geometrical designs of the Muslim world. In the 15th century Granada and Seville produced models which, from a technical and decorative point of view, were firmly rooted in traditional Moorish culture. The production from Granada stands out for its facings, particularly wall-cladding, involving the use of mosaics of varied geometrical forms, linked together in complex combinations. These monochrome plaques, employing colours obtained from several oxides applied over tin glazing, involved slow manufacture, and the laying techniques demanding highly skilled artisans. The export of tile-mosaics was almost out of the question.

This type of composition was also employed in Portugal, but solely at Sintra Palace. Santos Simões considered that the 'carpet' of the palace chapel and the floor of the so-called Dom Afonso IV Room involved manufacturing and laying techniques foreign to Spain. He thought that these examples of tile-mosaics were carried out in Sintra by Moorish artisans. Indeed, the widespread use of tiles in Portugal, particularly from the end of the 15th century, did not evolve from any local tradition. It can be supposed that general acceptance of the so-called 'Hispano-Moresque' tile, most of which were manufactured in Seville, was because King Manuel I saw this form of decoration during his visit in 1498 to Toledo and Saragossa with his wife, Dona Isabel, daughter of the Catholic Kings, when he was sworn in as heir to the thrones of Castile, Leon and Aragon. On this occasion he also visited Andalucia.

It was at his initiative that thousands of *azulejos* were laid in Sintra Palace, some of Portuguese manufacture, although most came from Seville. The variety of patterns and the use of different techniques in their decoration – *cuerda seca, cuenca, sgraffito* and relief tiles, the latter also employing the *cuerda seca* technique (see Glossary) – make the Sintra set of *azulejos* one of the most remarkable collections of all the Hispano-Moresque tiles. Here are the only examples of *cuerda seca* tiles bearing the armillary sphere, the King's emblem (illustration 28); the walls of the Arab Room are decorated with dynamic geometric designs simulating three-dimensionality and contrast with the relief motifs that are used as the surrounds (illustration 29); other rooms are ornamented with tiles in relief, vine-leaves that develop organic rhythms in opposed curves, forming 'carpets' interrupted by door surrounds that are made either of *cuerda seca*, relief or *sgraffito* tiles or of tile-mosaics (the latter in the Mermaid Room); there are also motifs of bows and stars (the Magpie Room).

Orders placed by the clergy, the principal customer for Seville tiles, were responsible for other spectacular revetments, some of which still exist. Coimbra's Old Cathedral, a 12th-century building, was throughout the first half of the 16th century covered with *azulejos* inside, particularly *cuenca tiles, mudéjar* decorated tiles and also, principally, Renaissance tiles. Piers were covered with *azulejos* overlaid in rings, walls were lined with 'carpets' enriched with concentric mouldings, other compositions simulated *couronnements* (see Glossary), windows, doors with lances, broken or trefoil arches and provided this ancient church with the most versatile decoration of its day. The versatility arose from the variety of solutions that mimicked buildings within the heavy Norman architecture itself, and their brilliance and designs gave life to the whole edifice. It was very different from the contemporary solutions of Andalucia, and it reflected the total freedom with which our tile-layers worked, since they were surely unaware of how the *azulejos* were laid, even in other parts of Portugal. For example in the Chapter House of the Conceição Convent in Beja, a city close to Andalucia, we can suppose that artisans from Seville would have come to lay the tiles that decorate the walls. The *cuerda seca* tiles in illustration 30 are from the convent at Beja and were inspired by the brocade fabrics of the times, and they were used to replace these luxurious and costly materials on the altar frontals. Other important examples of Hispano-Moresque tiles in buildings can be seen in the Church of São Paulo de Frades, Coimbra; in the crypt of the Church of Jesus, Setúbal, with its patterned *sgraffito* with an upper moulding bearing a Gothic inscription; and in the Quinta da Bacalhoa.

The National Museum of Azulejo has in its collection a great variety of Hispano-Moresque tiles employing various techniques that are representative of the various types of application: *cuerda seca* and *cuenca*, the majority of the latter from the Old Cathedral in Coimbra (illustration 34); *azulejos* with a pattern on just one tile and in combinations of tiles arranged 2 x 2; both *sgraffito* and lustre tiles (illustration 36); bearing *mudéjar* bow (illustration 31) and star motifs; pattern-decorated tiles in a Gothic style; floral motifs; figurative tiles in the Gothic tradition (illustrations 32 and 33), in relief (illustration 35), for floor and ceiling plaques (illustration 37); as well as a heraldic panel bearing the arms of the Dukes of Braganza (illustration 38). These examples cover the period from the last quarter of the 15th century to about 1550.

The Museum has another example of the arms of the Dukes of Braganza, dating from 1558 (illustration 39), which originated, as did illustration 38, at the palace of Vila Viçosa. While no. 38 from the early 16th century is in *cuenca*, no. 39 is one of the earliest examples in Portugal of majolica or faience tiles. It comes from a section of an ashlar that Duke Teodósio ordered from Flanders. Indeed, Flanders produced large quantities of ceramics and its ceramicists contributed much to the evolution of the *azulejo* on the Iberian Peninsula. At about the same time, some of these craftsmen settled in Seville and Talavera de la Reina and in Lisbon, where we know that several were already established in 1565. We can therefore surmise that by about 1560 majolica tile manufacture had started in Lisbon in the hands of Portuguese and Flemish craftsmen. This unique commission for Vila Viçosa, which was not followed up in the history of the *azulejo* in Portugal, was placed at a time of changing taste, when the majolica technique came to be definitively rooted in the manufacture of the *azulejo* and when the Mannerist style began to be adopted. Half a century earlier an Italian, Francisco Niculoso, had unsuccessfully endeavoured to introduce the production of majolica tiles to Seville, where he had settled.

Considering the short life of the Antwerp production, the Vila Viçosa panels are of great importance, both for the large number handed down to us and for their quality. This Italo-Flemish decoration is carried out in exquisitely precise miniature painting. The style, spread across Europe following the discovery of the Domus Aurea in Rome, consists of cartels, *cartouches*, grotesques, urns, garlands, fruit and animals painted over a yellow background and framed with shields, horsemen or phases in the life of Tobias. These important panels, recently attributed to the workshop of Den Salm, were removed from the palace rooms during the second half of the 19th century. The greater part was placed in another area of the palace. Of those that were dispersed, the Museum houses the section bearing the ducal arms

and another focused on a horseman within a circular moulding (illustration 40). The first Portuguese production of majolica, a little later than these Flemish panels, permitted the development of what we can consider national characteristics, in their scale, dimensions and perfect integration into buildings.

Of the Mannerist production of the second half of the 16th century, the panel of *Susannah and the Elders* (illustration 41), dating to about 1565, belonging to the Bacalhôa Palace, Azeitão, and the revetment of the São Roque Chapel in the church of the same name in Lisbon, designed by Francisco de Matos, of about 1584 (illustration 42) are outstanding. One of the masterpieces of that age is the panel of *Our Lady of Life*, attributed to Marçal de Matos, produced about 1580, which is now in the National Museum of Azulejo (illustration 43). This huge panel, consisting of 1,384 *azulejos*, is from the former parish church of St Andrew in Lisbon, near St George's Castle, which was partially demolished in 1845 due to town planning requirements. One of the parts of the church that was lost was the side chapel, founded and decorated by Bartolomeu Vaz de Lemos who died in 1580. The panel is thought to have lined the end wall of the chapel, and it is likely that the rectangular space now visible in the upper portion was the result of an enlargement of a window, the composition of the panel thus reflecting the gilded wooden retable of the same age. When the National Library (Biblioteca Nacional) was transferred to a recently erected building, the panel was once again dismantled and moved to the National Museum of Ancient Art where it was placed in the former Nativity Scene House (Casa do Presépio), an annexe of the St Anthony Chapel at the Madre de Deus Convent. The work undertaken on the building prior to the XVIIth Exhibition of Art, Science and Culture (1983) meant that the panel had to be moved once more. It was put on display in 1989, and in 1994 it was re-erected in a space created for the purpose and integrated into the scheme of the Museum where the Mannerist works of the 16th century are exhibited. The panel, measuring 5 m x 4.65 m, is a *trompe l'oeil* retable, the iconography of which is more than merely decorative. In addition to being a work that is instructional but also appeals to the feelings through its dramatic and pictorial qualities, it is one of the finest examples in the entire Portuguese output of wall ceramics. Four Corinthian columns arise from a pediment, decorated with diamond shapes, and divided into three parts, supporting an entablature ornamented with grotesques. At the sides niches holding the sculptural figures of the Evangelists St John and St Luke (illustration 44) draw the eye to the centre of the retable. Here, with a treatment that is frankly pictorial, is a large-scale scene of the Adoration of the Shepherds (illustration 45). Completing the retable at the top, a surrounding garland – recalling the moulding of ceramic medallions produced in Florence during the 15th and 16th centuries (illustration 7) – sets apart a perspective scene of an Annunciation (illustration 46). Essential to the scenographic effect of this retable, surely with its iconographic source in Flemish and Italian engravings, are erudite quotations from classical architecture, precise and academic detailing of the drawing and the excellent colour composition, which takes the greatest possible advantage of the limited range of colours used in majolica. The first great example of a revetment that disturbs the plane of the wall yet fully lines it, the panel of *Our Lady of Life* is typical of the originality of this art in Portugal, at a high point when principles of painting were being applied to wall ceramics.

Mannerism is defined as being anti-classical in spirit, and this is demonstrated in this retable in 'the capricious design, the figures delineated in serpentine lines and the theatrical postures'. But this style, which was easily disseminated through the widespread circulation of engravings, is also visible in the exotic and the irrational. The rectangular *azulejo* (illustration 47), which is part of the skirting of one of the rooms of the 'fresco house' at Quinta da Bacalhoa, represents a fantastic creature resting on a branch bearing fruits and flowers, regarded by a surprised monkey, an animal that is not European. The imagery here comes from Flemish engravings; the painting, which is fluid and rich in subtle hues, highlights the principal characteristics of the Portuguese *azulejo*, of which this piece, as is the greater part of the majolica painting at Quinta

da Bacalhoa, is one of the earliest examples.

During the last quarter of the 16th century there developed the solutions to problems or ornamentation that were to be used up to about 1670: compositions of grotesques that were employed by international Mannerism; repetitive 'carpet' patterns, including those that imitated fabrics; figurative panels; and, lastly, a new solution that involved low manufacturing costs for the covering of large areas of walls, the chequered *azulejo*. By the beginning of the 17th century academically trained artists no longer seem to have been involved in ceramic painting. The *azulejo* was now painted solely by artisans who transferred engravings in a rather ingenuous manner. This lack of erudition can clearly be seen in the decoration of the grotesques, in which the structure of the composition is simplified through symmetry and through the reduction of scale. The panels in the Sanctuary of the Espírito Santo Church in Évora (1631) are an example of the former, as are those of the narthex of the Santo Amaro hermitage in Lisbon, dating from about 1670. Examples of the latter are the panels of the São Bento Convent in Lisbon, now in the collection of this Museum. Lining the staircase of what had been one of the largest religious buildings in the capital, the panels, six in number, were manufactured during the second quarter of the 17th century. One of the oldest is dated 1630. This set of panels is distinguished from the rest of the Portuguese production of the time by the lozenge shape of the *azulejos*, the only shape that would allow organization of the reticle in a way that followed both vertical lines and lines parallel to the slope of the staircase. The panel in illustration 48 is filled with a network of designs in the centre of which the tower and the sun, symbols of Benedictine iconography, stand out within a cartel. Other cartels repeat a lion bearing a crosier and oval rosettes. In this network of volutes there is a fantastic profusion of griffins, birds of prey, and dogs emerging from acanthus leaves, all repeated, in addition to mitres resting on *cartouche* and small boys seated amid foliage or hidden among the scrolls of the cartels, masks, cherubs, plumed heads – all motifs taken from Flemish engravings.

Such decoration employing grotesques was not exclusive to religious buildings. This can be seen in the panel dating from the first half of the 17th century (illustration 49) bearing the arms of the Viscounts of Vila Nova de Cerveira. The arms on the cartel form the axis of the composition, developed symmetrically in volutes, *cartouche*, tridents, chimeras, leaves and fruits, cupids and dragons, on a panel that is landscape in shape but is suited to the decoration of rooms in a private palace.

Later examples of compositions similar to these large 16th-century panels are the 17th-century panels from the Santa Clare Convent in Évora (illustration 50). Of an 'experimental nature', according to Santos Simões, these panels recall once more the engravings produced in Flanders several decades earlier, in the great oval cartel, decorated in scrolls and *ferronerie*, containing a basket filled with fruit, plants and birds, a composition that is reminiscent of the decoration of altar frontals in the third quarter of the 17th century.

One of the most curious decorative solutions found for tiling large areas of walls in the 16th century involved the use of *azulejos* of two plain colours, white and green, set on the diagonal and placed alternately, as in a chess-board. The pertinence of the comment made by Santos Simões about chequered *azulejos* deserves repeating: '… the *azulejo*, even though bearing no painted ornament, has in itself plastic characteristics sufficient to determine decorative rhythms …' Indeed, '… the *azulejo*, or rather, the shape of the *azulejo*, determines its decorative potential, … the reticle is its greatest plastic value …' Now, when two colours of *azulejos* were used alternately, there was created, in addition to '… a rectilinear rhythm, a spatial rhythm in which the *azulejo* freed itself from its squareness to acquire an area …' Many revetments using, in addition to the white *azulejos*, green, blue and honey-coloured ones, in associations of two, three and even four colours, are still in existence. They reflect a certain variety of composition, and it is not unusual to find more than one on the same wall. Several of these solutions can be found at the Museum, such as those that, in keeping with similar principles, link *azulejos* to brick (floor skirting), or other geometri-

cal shapes such as triangles and trapezia (illustration 51).

Although the cost of producing chequered *azulejos* was low, laying them was a slow process that required skilled workers, which was also true of the old tile-mosaics. Use of the chequered tile was soon to be dropped for this reason, although it was remembered in the 'false chequers', in which square tiles simulated, in blue and white paintwork, various square and rectangular geometrical shapes. This can be seen in the St Clare Convent in Funchal, dating from the mid-17th century, which is also documented in the collection. In a natural process of evolution, and influenced by the patterned 'carpets' of the times, the 'frame' or 'chequered' compositions replaced the square white tiles with other ornamented ones. An example in the Museum of this 'composite' or 'rich chequering' scheme is the complete lining of the original Cloister (illustration 3). Pattern tiles became more usual during the 17th century, particularly on walls, and they were also employed to line vaults, domes and altar frontals. The chequered *azulejo* imposed powerful, dynamic diagonal rhythms, and this was also true of the pattern-tiles when the centres of the modules and the oblique layout of the motifs were alternated, suggesting rotation.

There were several reasons for the success of this product, which was chiefly manufactured by the Lisbon workshops but also, to a lesser extent, by those of Coimbra and Oporto: the diversity of the decoration, in general of Italo-Flemish origin although also incorporating other tastes foreign to the European tradition; ease of manufacture and low cost due to repetition; and the natural juxtaposition of several patterns in the same building.

Imposing for their colour, rhythm and the sheer size of the area they occupied, the patterns linked variety of application to their own diversity. Patterns based on 2 x 2, 4 x 4, 6 x 6 or even 12 x 12 modules could be laid side by side on the same surface, separated by frames. Doorways and window-openings picked out by borders were used to avoid a certain monotony caused by excessive repetition. Patterns based on a smaller module were usually reserved for the lower portions of the walls, the larger ones being applied to surfaces farther from the eye of the viewer. The monumental nature that characterizes the Portuguese *azulejo* is clearly seen in these many and varied solutions. The cladding generally rises from floor-level to ceiling, even lining vaults. Constituting more that just a decorative adjunct to the architecture, the pattern-*azulejo* transfigures the space and creates diffuse surroundings.

One of the earliest examples of pattern-*azulejos* in majolica was produced in Lisbon around 1565. They were made for the Quinta da Bacalhoa (illustration 52). The radial geometric rhythms and the interwoven motifs reflect the *mudéjar* tradition of Seville, a compromise of taste with the new so-called Pisa technique that can be seen in other patterns of the times.

One of the more widespread Mannerist repetitive motifs in the Portuguese *azulejo* between the end of the 16th century and about 1630 was the 'diamond-tip' (illustration 53). The earliest of these originated in Seville although they were manufactured in Lisbon from the beginning of the following century. A pattern that recurred in Iberian manufacture, with many variants in Portugal, was what is known as Italo-Flemish (illustration 54). Its design was based on floor decoration in the Italian Renaissance, where cross-shaped and hexagonal tiles were frequently used together. However, to simplify manufacturing procedures assemblages of several forms of tiles were reduced to just one simple *azulejo*.

The vine-leaf pattern in illustration 55 which had originated in Talavera de la Reina was created by the ceramicist Juan Fernandez to fulfil an order from Philip II for the Escorial Monastery. This pattern was also produced in Seville and Lisbon but, despite its beauty, it was only applied during the first quarter of the 17th century. More common in Portugal was the so-called quatrefoil pattern, in use up to the end of the 17th century (illustration 56), a pattern formed by 4 x 4 tiles, visually very imposing. Its definition was exceptionally clear, even when viewed from a distance, and it was therefore often used to form 'carpets' in the higher parts of walls.

The influence of the Orient was apparent in the repetitive *azulejos*, and one of the pattern 'families' that was most widely used, with spectacular results, was the 'camellia family'; this was the general name given by Santos Simões to the flower represented in Oriental porcelain either by the rose or by the magnolia. It was produced, with many variations, in sets of 2 x 2 and 4 x 4 (illustration 57) and was used between about 1640 and the end of the 17th century, although only in blue. One of the links is formed by a small flower and two facing carnations emerging from a tulip, while the other consists of the large flower that gave its name to the pattern. The use of manganese and green, together with blue and yellow – the more common colours – renders this variation one of the most beautiful examples of the 'camellia'. It was used in the Church of São Luis Gonzaga in Pinhel, on a panel 46 tiles in height, and its parallel can be seen in the refectory of the former convent of St Joan (Santa Joana) in Aveiro, now a museum (illustration 58), where the entire wall is covered in pattern-tiles, this time bordered with scrolls.

The large patterned 'carpets' also incorporated emblematic, hagiographic and narrative panels that replaced oils on canvas. Although there are churches in which the entire walls are lined in pattern-tiles, there are also countless examples of tiles bearing symbolic representations and of series formed by precise iconographic designs conceived as 'paintings'. Also numerous are emblematic panels depicting a monstrance, symbol of the Eucharist. The monstrance sometimes stands alone or, more frequently, is flanked by angels and clouds or resting on an altar (illustration 19). Of the hagiographic panels, those depicting Our Lady in various forms – Our Lady of Rosário, Our Lady of Boa Viagem and Our Lady of Ajuda – are outstanding, as are those depicting saints, particularly those that were more popular among the faithful – for example St Anthony, of Lisbon – and the complete series of the Apostles. A small panel from a series showing the *Life of Our Lady* depicts St Anne and St Joachim as part of a patterned 'carpet' consisting of white and yellow quatrefoils intertwined with acanthus leaves (illustration 59). To execute this figurative panel, the artist used an engraving as a model and he was able to produce an ingenuous and powerfully expressive image. The forms of the figures and the background architecture are heightened by chiaroscuro, used here to organize the image visually and not to give a mimetic effect of representation. Several works by artisans, charming for their ingenuousness, include those representing *St James* (illustration 60), *St John the Evangelist* (illustration 61) and the *Holy Family* (illustration 62).

Two panels in particular are surprising for their scale, colour and decorative richness: the central motif focuses on a flowered *albarrada* (see Glossary), vases decorated with masks and garlands borne on satyrs and flanked, one by angels (illustration 63) and the other by parrots (illustration 64). These were part of a group lining the walls of the former convent of Nossa Senhora da Esperança, in Lisbon. Seventeenth-century thinkers and poets meditated on the symbolic meaning of the flowers, linked to the theological virtue of Hope, of which these panels are an iconographic transcription. In addition to their decorative effect, these panels are historically the first use of a motif that was very successful in *azulejo* manufacture before the middle of the 18th century. While in this group each *albarrada* forms a separate panel with its own frame, from the end of the 17th century the vase with flowers was to be used as a motif in series, placed alternately with other motifs – such as balustrades and dolphins – and surrounded by scrolls of leaves. An example of this ornamental design can be seen on the walls of the Large Cloister in the *albarradas* that date from the first half of the 18th century, placed here at the time of the extensive reconstruction towards the end of last century.

The 17th-century panels of *albarradas* once again reveal a debt to Flemish engraving, also the source for altar frontals known as 'birds and foliage'. These frontals, which betray influences from the East, were mostly produced in Lisbon. They constitute a most interesting piece of evidence of transmigration of culture in Portuguese decorative art. The centres of greatest significance are in the Alentejo, in the Lisbon region and in the Azores. Santos Simões believed that their decoration was taken from the printed cotton fabrics brought from India by the Portuguese. There is no proof of this, because of the frailty of the fabrics, but other cloths of a later date, also Indian, bear a resemblance to these frontals, which were also inspired, to a certain extent, by cheap embroidery, Indo-Portuguese furniture and Mogul miniatures. The structure of the design of these frontals was identical: it consisted of a central 'panel' bearing figures and a framework in Renaissance style. There are, however, variations: the frontals can be composed of a whole 'panel' (illustration 66) or one divided into two or three (illustration 65); the figures of exotic or European fauna consist of land animals at the lower level and, higher up, of birds either flying or resting on branches of trees bearing leaves or fruit (peacocks appear in greater numbers); the figures can be delineated with considerable freedom or kept strictly symmetrical; the design can also be centred on coats-of-arms or saints set in cartels. The trees are reminiscent of representations of the Tree of Life, while the peacocks signify, in Christian symbolism, Christ's Resurrection and the immortality of the soul.

The Portuguese despatched *azulejos* to their colonies beyond Europe, especially to Brazil. During the sea voyage the tiles served as ships' ballast. It was more difficult to transport them to India because of the length of the voyage and because the space was required for more important cargoes. Thus it was that when Goa wanted to decorate the floors and walls of the church of the St Monica Convent, local tiles were used, made somewhere on the Indian subcontinent. The decoration of these tiles (illustrations 67 and 68) is similar to none produced in Portugal. Rather, it is the result of a need for a tradition to be observed – the lining of buildings by ceramics – and use was made of decorative arabesque motifs of Persian origin, widely employed throughout the Muslim world. Use was also made of the Tree of Life which, associated in the East with fecundity, had its parallel in Christian symbolism in the Tree of the Cross of Christ, whose death is the source of life.

Following a period under Spanish rule (1580-1640), Portugal once again gained its independence. The nobility, called upon to play a role in court life, now wanted to decorate their palaces, no longer in the Mannerist style that prevailed in the churches, with pattern-tiles. They sought, moreover, Flemish sources, profane themes such as mythological, satirical or hunting scenes. An example of this new taste is a panel that represents, over a background of nature, the *Triumph of Amphitrite and Poseidon* (illustration 69), a classical theme suited to the new requirements for ostentation. Referring back to erudite imagery, the artist endeavoured to transpose it 'correctly' but because of his lack of an academic training, the result is an ingenuous work, although strong and full of character. In a panel dating from the third quarter of the 17th century (illustration 70) the satire is developed through the portrayal of animals busy in activities usually reserved to human beings, against a background of a city of tall towers: a chicken is driven in a coach drawn by a monkey; a triumphal carriage pulled by horses accommodates monkeys playing musical instruments. Its discourse is corrosive and such scenes were usually linked to panel pictures decorating such leisure areas as palace gardens. This panel, from a country house far from any urban centre, is similar to others at the Fronteira Palace which, in the 17th century, lay outside Lisbon. The work of craftsmen, it depicts festivities, scenes similar to Dutch genre painting and satirical Flemish engravings.

A hunting scene (illustration 71) has its source in similar Flemish engraving. Hunting was the activity that occupied the greater part of the nobility's entertainment. Inspired by an engraving by J. Collaert, after a drawing by Johannes Stradanus, the panel-picture represents a leopard-hunt in which it is supposed that a female leopard could be caught by using a trap baited with a mirror, a temptation which the leopardess would be unable to resist. While keeping to the spatial design, the painter changed the representation of the hunters, replacing Europeans with half-naked negroes, clothed only with feather loin-cloths, the exoticism being further enhanced by a palm tree in the foreground. This represented the Portuguese view of the peoples of their empire.

A polychrome scene even more provoking than those of the previous panels can be seen in the designs decorated with hunting scenes between animals (illustrations 18 and 72). In zones marked out by acanthus scrolls which, in the larger panels, develop into interlaced volutes, animals are shown chasing each other: dogs attack bulls and lions, a deer is chased by dogs or a cat faces a mouse. Though the large cartels that depict scenes follow Mannerist examples of the 16th century, the graphic representation using moulding is not maintained and there has been an organic development of forms, pointing the way to the baroque.

Contemporary Portuguese faience production, which until then had employed only blue and manganese, and the possible influence of Dutch tiles that were painted solely in blue and white, may have led to a break in the use of polychromy in *azulejo* manufacture, of which these panels were the final examples. The process involving changes in taste during the 1660s and 1670s can be seen in the extraordinary group of wall ceramics in the palace of the Marquises of Fronteira (illustration 73), the most important example of lay architecture of the 1600s.

The portraits of *Charles II of England* and his wife, *Catherine of Braganza*, are painted in blue on rectangular tiles, perhaps of English manufacture. They were made at the time of their marriage in 1662 (illustrations 74 and 75). Tile-painting only in blue became fashionable in Portugal about 1690. At the same time, new tastes developed in a monarchy and in a society that began to respond to the fashions that were spreading out from Versailles across the whole of Europe.

New developments were taking place in the production of Portuguese tiles, the contribution of Gabriel del Barco being considerable. Born in Spain and having settled in Portugal in 1669, del Barco began working as a painter. He decorated ceilings with great volutes of foliage, using a two-dimensional treatment similar to that of the picture-panel tiles of hunting scenes (see above). During the closing decade of the 17th century he began to paint only *azulejos* and he left a body of work remarkable both for its quantity and for the innovations that he introduced. A novelty that was to have the greatest consequences was the 'pictorial' treatment, in which his brush-strokes were obvious, a departure made possible by the painting in blue alone, free from the constraints imposed by outline drawing in manganese. This is clear in the basket of flowers with its ample surround in illustration 76.

Attributed to Gabriel del Barco and dating from about 1700 is the *Great View of Lisbon*, a panel measuring 23 m in length. It shows the city spread out along the River Tagus, in the European tradition of the *vedute*, much seen in engravings, impressive in this case for its sheer size. The panel, produced about 50 years before the great earthquake (1755) that razed Lisbon, is therefore of even greater importance for it shows – although with no concern for relative scale nor exact detailing – many of the buildings that suffered the effects of the earthquake. Some of those and areas depicted in the panels are: Belém Tower and the Jerónimos Monastery (illustration 78), the Santo Amaro Hermitage; the Santos-o-Velho Church, the São Bento Convent and the Mocambo District, location of the *azulejo* workshops (illustration 80), the churches of Santa Catarina, Loreto and São Roque (illustration 79), Terreiro do Paço (illustration 77), the Cathedral, the Castle and the São Vicente de Fora Monastery, the Casa dos Bicos, the d'El Rei Fountain, the church of Santa Engrácia; and the church of Madre de Deus (illustration 17). The panel also shows Lisbon's main palaces that can be seen from the river and public buildings such as the Customs House and the Arsenal; such features as markets, fountains, bridges, shipping on the Tagus, shipyards and land transport; it is an invaluable source of precious information about the capital at the beginning of the 18th century.

During the last quarter of the 17th and early 18th centuries the Portuguese imported from Holland monumental groups of tile panels. These are still to be found, in the main, in the buildings for which they were designed, including the Madre de Deus Convent itself. The convent houses several panels by Jan van Oort (illustration 8) and one by Willem van der Kloet. The popularity of Dutch tiles in Portugal was due to a recognition of their technical superiority. To a certain extent they were adapted to Portuguese taste, for example in their monumental size, which is much larger than the usual Dutch tiles pro-

duced for domestic consumption. Many of these Dutch panels in Portugal are religious, but the Museum has an example designed for a palace: a dancing class in a garden, painted with a strict regard for perspective, in which the personages are distributed in a classically balanced arrangement (illustration 81); it formed part of a group of scenes depicting the leisure of the aristocracy. Dutch competition in supplying more refined designs and an exquisite technique caused a natural reaction: the Portuguese not only understood that they had to improve the quality of their tiles, but they also saw that the new demands could not be met by production in the hands of artisans. As a result painters with academic training, used to painting on canvas, were asked to paint *azulejos*. The vigorous brushwork and spontaneity of Gabriel del Barco made up, to a certain extent, for his limitations in matters of composition and drawing. The creation of monumental assemblages is indebted to him, specially those designed for churches, which sometimes covered entire walls with dynamic compositions accentuated by a powerful framework, and also the mythological-scene panels designed for palace decorations (illustration 82).

Another new departure, for it had not been seen in 17th-century production, was that on many occasions the painters began to sign their works, sure of their status as artists. These masters of the first half of the 18th century were to contribute to the triumph of the baroque in the production of the *azulejo* for numerous monumental assemblages throughout Portugal and also in Brazil. Although in several artists' works direct Dutch influence can be detected, more sensual pictorial values predominated, together with impressive architectural backgrounds and the perfect integration of the panels into larger surfaces. The excellent work of Manuel dos Santos and António Pereira made them famous at the beginning of the century, but it was Master António de Oliveira Bernardes who dominated and many of the artists of the next generation were to pass through his workshop. Fortunately, the principal collections of the work of these artists is still preserved in the buildings for which they were conceived. The Museum, however, in addition to an exceptional group attributed to Manuel dos Santos, has several examples of this so-called 'cycle of the Master' type, very individual in character, such as the *Flight into Egypt* (illustration 83), a small panel which is a fragment of a larger composition by Policarpo de Oliveira Bernardes, son of António, and his disciple. There is also a 'marine' scene (illustration 85), framed by pilasters, volutes, garlands and caryatids, which render the composition extremely scenographic; this is also a work personalized by the hand of a master. In 1994 the Museum acquired an important group by an artist known as Master PMP, whose monogram can be seen on his works. They have an ingenuousness, are always very descriptive and reveal a taste for scenes of gallantry, not frequently found in Portuguese painting at that time.

During the second quarter of the 18th century, the output of *azulejos* probably increased considerably to meet the greater demand in the decoration of new buildings and the redecoration of old ones. Many orders were also received from Brazil, where the market was developing quickly. It was at this time that the largest sets of *azulejos* ever to be made in Portugal were applied, one at the monastery of São Vicente de Fora in Lisbon and the other at the monastery of St Francis, in Salvador da Bahia, in Brazil. This was the 'Great Production cycle' linked to masters such as Teotónio dos Santos, Valentim de Almeida and, particularly, Bartolomeu Antunes and his son-in-law, Nicolau de Freitas. These are the most outstanding names, but there were many anonymous artisans who carried out correct, often stereotyped work and were capable of creating wide scenographic backgrounds but more as a result of their themes than for their originality or vigour of painting (illustrations 87 and 88). Spaces that reveal theatrical scenes and frames that are 'cut out' at the top (illustration 86) hold compositions drawn in short brush-stokes and done in washes; they manage to create a refined atmosphere with small figures against a background of a port or a garden – in fishing or hunting scenes, narrating stories without history. *Azulejo* manufacture was also developing at Coimbra at this time, in an exaggerated baroque style of which the Museum houses an example bearing Our Lady of Life, dated 1750.

Parallel with the production of these large figurative panels, other types of *azulejo* were made in increasing numbers. Examples include the *albarradas*, already mentioned, and free-standing figures indebted to Dutch influences. Portugal also imported from The Netherlands tiles decorated with autonomous miniature scenes, applied in a 'national' style, that is, with a surround, in keeping with tradition. With Portuguese tiles normally measuring 14 x 14 cm, a new size of tile had to be made measuring 13 x 13 cm in order to frame the imported material (illustration 90). Production of the Portuguese free-standing figure tiles, generally made by young apprentices, was widespread and was intended to be cheaper, so they could be applied in the subsidiary areas of lay and religious buildings, such as corridors and kitchens; this explains their ingenuous character.

This range of production, from which the pattern-tile was generally absent, defines mid-century output, including the great narrative cycles for churches, leisure scenes for palaces (illustration 20) or genre scenes for gardens (illustration 89) and small devotional panels of a more intimate nature (illustration 93). Still applied during the baroque period, the *azulejo* altar frontal (illustration 92) disappeared, for it was impossible to apply tiles to the new forms of rococo altars.

In the middle of the 18th century the almost exclusive predominance of cobalt blue, used over the preceding 60 years, came to an end. Other colours were once more introduced in *azulejo* painting. Exquisite examples include the two Sacristy panels of the Madre de Deus Church, made between 1746 and 1749 (illustration 9), which also demonstrate the evolution of the design of the surrounds to organic foliage forms, which replaced the voluminous architectural types still to be seen in the panels made around 1740-5 for the St Anthony Chapel (illustration 6).

The decorative vocabulary of the rococo was established about 1750-5 and was maintained until about 1780-90 in a great variety: conches, larger or smaller, with sinuous leaves; designs painted just in blue (illustration 94), and others in polychrome for the surround and blue or manganese in the centre (illustrations 95 and 98). The finest examples of the richness achieved in the solutions in the art of the *azulejo* of the second half of the 18th century can be seen in the gardens of the Quinta do Azulejo in Lisbon and at Queluz Palace (illustration 102). The devotional panels provide a curious display of the rococo *azulejo*: hagiographic panels had been applied to the outside of lay buildings since the beginning of the 18th century, but the earthquake of 1755 led to the multiplication of these displays of religious sentiment. The devotional panels, generally in cut-out tiles, are dedicated to the more popular saints, such as St Anthony of Lisbon, and to the protectors against calamities, such as St Marçal and St Francis Borgia. Others have a more complex design, bearing images of Our Lady with Saints (illustration 95). Along the same lines, *alminhas*, small panels representing souls in purgatory for whom passers-by should pray, were popular subjects for public worship (illustration 96).

In about 1730, cut-out figures of men, on *azulejos* ('Welcome figures'), were placed along the staircase of the Santo Antão do Tojal Palace, near Lisbon, guiding visitors on their way through the building. Use of this kind of decoration increased throughout the century, employing figures that were generally of men, military figures which, during the second half of the century, came to be dressed in a somewhat exotic fashion (illustration 97).

Although the Museum's collections are almost exclusively made up of Portuguese *azulejos*, or of foreign tiles used in Portugal, it was thought that comparison with those produced abroad could help in providing a better understanding of this art which, to a greater or lesser extent, was also practised in other countries. This has led to the formation of a nucleus of foreign tiles, naturally smaller in number, of which the English tile made in Bristol around 1760-70 (illustration 99), a contemporary of the items referred to above, is a good example.

During the second half of the century, the pattern tradition of the 1600s was taken up once more, as a cheap, expeditious way to decorate the buildings that were being put up after the 1755 earthquake. This type of tile is known as *Pombaline*, the name taken from the Marquis of Pombal, Prime Minister

to King José I, who was responsible for rebuilding the city. The patterns are very decorative, despite discretion in colour and design. They were generally laid alternately, first an *azulejo* with a radial motif (rosette), then another with an 'X' motif, its corners decorated to establish the link. On other occasions the design would consist of the repetition of a single motif contained on just one *azulejo*, for example illustration 100. In this case, the repetition of the motif created a grid, through dark and light areas, simulating the incidence of light. This illusion of volume became imperceptible in neo-classical patterns, which are clearly linear in design. Once again, as was the case with the 'carpets' of earlier centuries, there is always a border, here decorated with plumes arranged in undulating rhythms. We also owe to the Marquis of Pombal the reformation of university studies in Coimbra, and larger than usual *azulejos* were made for the university, well suited to a new and objective educational purpose (illustration 101).

Towards the end of the century, during the 1780s, neo-classical ornamentation was gradually adopted in *azulejo* decoration. A late arrival, this style created many fine decorative tiles, particularly at the Real Fábrica do Rato, set up in 1767 to provide fine pottery ware, which was already making rococo *azulejos*.

The Museum has many fine examples of neo-classicism that reflect the influence of the frescoes of Pompeii or the engravings of designs by Robert and James Adam. Outstanding is the flanked ashlar dating from about 1800. The main panel is centred on an urn and is composed symmetrically of eagles bearing crowns and flowered garlands, in a classical style that is contrasted in a baroque revival by the dolphins at the base (illustrations 103 and 104). From this same period, probably also produced at the Fábrica do Rato, is a group of seven panels recounting episodes from the life of António Joaquim Carneiro, a hatter, from his poor childhood working in the fields as a shepherd to an adult life of prosperity (illustrations 105 to 110). These panels recount his ascent up the social ladder in a self-congratulatory biography, for the panels were laid in his own house.

The confidence of the bourgeoisie, linked to trade

and industry and the result of the economic policy begun by Pombal, was to be re-asserted following the period of the French invasions, the departure of the royal family to Brazil and the civil war, which ended in 1833. A few years later, new pottery and tile factories were established. The period of crisis suffered by ceramic and tile producers had come to an end and the *azulejo* was once more in demand in the towns. Again the traditional pattern-tile was popular, although now used to clad building façades with a brilliance, colour and rhythm that recall the virtues of the *azulejo* in previous centuries. Factories, both large and small, mushroomed in Lisbon and in the Oporto area, developing semi-industrial and industrial production practices. Decoration techniques included stencilling and stamping. There was often a preference for relief tiles in the north (illustration 112), made at the Massarelos and Devezas factories during the last quarter of the century. In Lisbon the highest output came from the Viúva Lamego and Sacavém factories. The latter was English-owned, and imported clays, oxides and models from Great Britain. It was particularly involved in stamped tiles and, later, in the semi-relief (illustration 119), revealing a taste for *Art Nouveau* (illustration 118).

Although the production of repetitive tiles was economical and led to a cheaper product, unique works continued to be made. One of the more renowned figures of this period, who had begun his career in the Fábrica do Rato, which closed down in 1835, was Luís Ferreira, better known as Ferreira das Tabuletas (or 'Sign-writer'). He became the art manager of Fábrica Viúva Lamego, and there he decorated the façade in 1865, with an ingenuous *trompe l'oeil* of vases of flowers and allegorical figures. Other important works of his that have been handed down to us include the interior of the Trindade beerhouse and exteriors such as that of a building in Largo Rafael Bordalo Pinheiro (illustration 113), in a Romantic style. The Museum houses several of his works: four columns surmounted by masonic symbols painted in blue (illustration 115) from the private garden of a house that had belonged to a wealthy member of the freemasons from Gallicia, and a polychrome vase of flowers

(illustration 114) from the same source.

Production in the Romantic style was to have several eclectic followers, among whom Pereira Cão (1841–1921) was pre-eminent. He was also art director of the Fábrica Viúva Lamego towards the end of the 19th century, and he was commissioned by Liberato Telles to make the two panels alluding to the life of St Auta, which were to be placed in the Madre de Deus Church (see illustration 117). Another famous artist who cultivated the production of historical subjects until a late date was Jorge Colaço (1868-1942). Beginning ceramics painting at the start of the 20th century, Colaço turned out imposing work, often endeavouring to transpose oil painting techniques to ceramics. Examples of this are the decoration of the Buçaco Palace Hotel near Coimbra, the Jácome Correia Palace in Ponta Delgada on the Azores, the stations at Évora and Beja and of São Bento in Oporto and the panels that now adorn the Carlos Lopes Pavilion in Lisbon. Here we show the panel commemorating the *Battle of Ourique* (illustration 116), the project for which was drawn up by the Museum. This type of work in Romantic style was applied during the 20th century at many railway stations and markets, depicting local people and monuments, the scenes being based on picture-postcard photographs. An example of the use of photography as a source of iconography is shown here in a popular image of the last Portuguese king (illustration 121). A taste for Naturalism, which had been depicted in Portuguese art since the end of the 19th century, now appeared in the *azulejo*, on which were represented landscapes, rural customs and traditions. This can be seen in the plaque by J. Costa, on which a woman teaches a child (illustration 122).

The work of Rafael Bordalo Pinheiro (1846–1905) was essential to the renaissance of ceramics and the *azulejo*. Setting up the Fábrica de Faianças das Caldas da Rainha in 1884, he produced a vast output. Technically well made, with enamels giving beautiful effects, and eclectic in his sources, he created naturalist forms in keeping with the forms created by Bernard Palissy (*c.* 1510–*c.* 90), which had inspired potters in several countries. At the same time he produced relief *azulejos* in a revival of the most beautiful of the Seville patterns of the first half of the 16th century, as one at Quinta da Bacalhoa (illustration 120).

'Use of the *azulejo* is the means most often employed to lend a touch of *Art Nouveau* to a somewhat indifferent façade', wrote Manuel Rio de Carvalho in 1986; indeed the movement was not very well understood in Portugal. Some of the wealthier bourgeoisie had some knowledge of it, which is apparent in their imports of *fin-de-siècle* tiles (illustration 123). Understood or not, and in an output that was sometimes eclectic (illustration 124), the *azulejo* made in the spirit of *Art Nouveau* is a part of Portuguese shop decoration, with its figurative panels, and is displayed on façades, in friezes and on platband revetments. At the turn of the century Rafael Bordalo Pinheiro was the ceramicist most in tune with this new spirit. Until the end of his life he turned out beautiful animal designs in relief, including grasshoppers (illustration 126) and butterflies (illustration 125), used in the decoration of bakeries, with greater affinity to the organic forms of contemporary French or Belgian products than to those of Anglo-Saxon countries (illustrations 127 and 128). This style was seen in the numerous, discrete patterns of the wall-tiles, most of which were manufactured at the Fábrica de Louça de Sacavém, in earthenware, sometimes copying English models (illustration 129), in slight relief and glazed in one (illustration 130) or two colours. Façades fully lined in *Art Nouveau azulejos* generally combine pattern-tiles with polychrome friezes bearing sinuous decorations of flowers and birds. The revetment designed by Alfredo Pinto (b. 1850) in 1911 (illustration 131) for the façade of a building in Avenida Almirante Reis in Lisbon is therefore an exception in that it was an overall composition created for a particular building.

In 1915, architect Raul Lino (1879-1974) designed a pattern for an *azulejo* in low relief for his 'Cypress House' in Sintra (illustration 132). His 'geometrism' – recalled in Austrian *Art Nouveau* and seen also in other designs (illustration 133) that were to be manufactured only for the retrospective exhibition dedicated to him in 1970 – was not followed up and had no immediate effect on Port-

uguese production, then more in tune with the more organic values of *Art Nouveau* and even with the Naturalism of the 1800s. It was only the industrial production in the 1930s of the Lusitânia (illustration 135) and the Sacavém (illustration 134) factories that was to use *Art Deco* patterns in strict designs that were almost always abstract, and made using tube-line techniques or aerography (see Glossary).

A restrained Modernism, supported by António Ferro, Portugal's cultural ideologue at the time of the great international exhibitions, found its inspiration in the motifs from 'folk art'. *Lambrilhas*, or miniature tiles, were made for the Paris International Exhibition of 1937 by several artists: Paulo Ferreira, Fred Kradolfer and Emmérico Nunes, in keeping with this spirit (illustration 136). Paulo Ferreira also designed for the same exhibition a first Modernist panel containing an aerial, fantasized view of Lisbon. This panel has disappeared, although a replica is now in the collection of the Museum (illustration 24).

Jorge Barradas (1894–1971) was 20th-century Portugal's most important designer of *azulejos*. Since the 1930s he worked continuously as a ceramicist, producing large panels for buildings. Important for the stimulus he gave to ceramics, Barradas made use in his work of motifs taken from other decorative art forms (illustration 137), in which his attachment to Mannerist and Baroque decoration is apparent. From his time, Fábrica Viúva Lamego was to welcome a new generation of ceramicists who collaborated with architects committed to experimenting with the new plastic techniques.

Maria Keil (b. 1914) was concentrating her attention on the *azulejo* when in 1957 she was given the opportunity to design large wall panels for the Metropolitano in the Lisbon underground stations. To be consistent with her concept that the *azulejo* is 'essentially a presence, a brilliance', she designed large, non-figurative revetments, based on the fact that a hurried passenger does not stop to contemplate a wall but rather gains a fleeting impression in passing of the *azulejos*. Even though she turned to the ancient techniques such as the *cuerda seca* (illustration 139) and even though the onlooker registers the coloured brightness of the façades (illustration

138), the *azulejo* now, in its modern context, assumes the dimension of pure form. Her collaboration with the Lisbon Metropolitano continued to 1972. In more recent commissions, a range of other artists have devised in their own styles a variety of spaces lined with *azulejos*, and the Museum houses a considerable core of panels designed by artists such as Sá Nogueira (b. 1921), Júlio Pomar (b. 1926), Vieira da Silva (1908–92), Eduardo Nery (b. 1938) and Manuel Cargaleiro (b. 1927; see illustrations 23, 140 and 142). The last, who has produced work continuously over a period, has a different attitude towards the *azulejo*, considering it as a support for painting. It is in this spirit that he has designed large spatial compositions, using loosely formed strokes and luminous chromatism. His work demonstrates his respect for tradition in both its freedom and decoration, as in the panel which, not without a certain irony, displays on its front the numbers and letters that on the back of the tile mark its relative position in the composition (illustration 141).

A strict 'geometrism' characterizes the work of another figure of the 1950s. Artur José is the author of smaller compositions exploring the expressiveness of ceramic material in elegant formalism (illustration 143).

The presence of the *azulejo* perceived purely as optical illusion, as Maria Keil pointed out, is suited to Eduardo Nery's visual explorations, which he developed even further on formal geometric compositions arranged in a chromatic grading of plain tiles linked to fragments of old, recovered *azulejos* (illustration 144). João Abel Manta (b. 1928), too, articulates the optical development of large surfaces with remembrances of walls containing *azulejos* from old panels dispersed and re-laid in random fashion (illustration 145).

A landmark of Portuguese ceramics in the second half of the 20th century is the work of Querubim Lapa (b. 1925) who has recently revisited tradition, creating spatial virtuality with the old chequering techniques (illustration 146), making good use of glazing and enamels, knowledge of which he has acquired over a long period. Querubim's updating of ancestral ceramic techniques has a link with the history of the Portuguese *azulejo* that is different from

that of Luís Pinto Coelho (b. 1932), who re-uses one of its most characteristic features, the 'welcome' figures (illustration 147), painted in emblematic blue and white, although described with troubled and absurd anatomies. Curious, and still within this link with the past, is the assimilation that Arnold Zimmerman (b. 1954) has made with Portuguese culture. This can be seen in his *azulejo* panel (illustration 148), in which symbols for events in his personal history are associated, in summary, with others from Portuguese history, some of which are linked to the very history of the *azulejo* itself, such as the silhouette of the Royal Palace at Sintra which King Manuel I ordered to be lined, five hundred years earlier, with one of the earliest and most sumptuous sets of *azulejos*.

The National Museum of Azulejo extends its natural sphere of interest to the study and display of other ceramic objects. In addition to regular exhibitions dealing with the output both of ceramicists and factories, its collections must include a nucleus of ceramics other than wall panels. Other museums in the capital and throughout the country have large collections of ancient Portuguese ceramics. However, these collections rarely include items later than the 19th century. Artistic interchange between three-dimensional ceramics and the *azulejo* explains the fact that the permanent exhibition contains the occasional item illustrating this cross-influence. These pieces are either on loan from other museums or belong to the Museum's own collection.

The expressive techniques of 17th-century ceramics are transposed to the *azulejo* in the outlining of shapes in manganese and also in what is still a late-Mannerist decorative feature, an evident taste for reflecting Eastern cultures. Following this type of output by unknown artists, the 18th century, chiefly through the Real Fábrica do Rato, produced articles both sumptuary and of daily use, as in the case of the beautiful urn with a floral decoration in *rocaille* (illustration 150), bearing the monogram of Tomás Brunetto, manager of the factory between 1767 and 1774.

On a par with the Romantic taste for lining walls with figurative compositions, there developed ceramics that had in the work of Wenceslau Cifka (1811-83), a Bohemian who came to Portugal with Ferdinand, the Prince Consort, an erudite expressiveness in elaborate forms and rich decoration. These were inspired by Renaissance ceramics, with which Cifka associated, rather eclectically, a historicist iconography of mythology and kings (illustration 151). The very *fin de siècle* neo-baroque centrepiece (illustration 152) was also a sign of the eclecticism and renewed vitality of Portuguese ceramics led by Rafael Bordalo Pinheiro. This was shortly to be brought up to date with elegant *Art Nouveau* objects that were in step with his relief *azulejo* work.

In line with a persistent current of historicist revivalism, the ceramics produced during the early decades of the 20th century repeated traditional forms and decoration. Jorge Barradas broke away during the 1930s and progressed along a Modernist path. With this style predominant, he produced, on a par with his *azulejo* work, ceramic objects, reliefs and wall sculptures. He also created small figurines in silhouette in the Mannerist style modelled both directly and moulded (illustration 153). At about the same time, Hein Semke (1899–1995), a German who had settled in Portugal, played a considerable role in Portuguese art, and became known for a dra-

matic expressionism and for an informal exploration of materials which can be seen in the ceramic plaque in illustration 154, dating from the 1960s.

It was also during this period of rediscovery of the uses of *azulejo* in buildings that a new modernization of Portuguese ceramics appeared in the wake of Jorge Barradas. One of the leading exponents of this trend was Querubim Lapa, whose work, even today, constitutes a strong link with traditions in ceramics. This is true of the plaque bearing a female mask, a reference to Japanese culture (illustration 155).

The more recent nucleus of the Museum has been built up of pieces made by artists whose work is pertinent to contemporary aesthetics. This is true of *A Tribute to Tàpies* by Maria João Oliveira (b. 1946; illustration 156), of *Diptych* by Cecília de Sousa (b. 1937; illustration 158), a vibrant ceramic object in which is revealed evidence of her work, which is largely made up of wall tiling. Examples of the work of the younger generation include the large vase (illustration 157) by Suzana Barros (b. 1961).

In this way, the National Museum of Azulejo meets its fundamental obligation of putting on display contemporary ceramics by distinguished artists.

João Castel-Branco Pereira

25
Ceramic floor tiles. Portugal?, 15th-16th
centuries
13.5; 7.8; 9.5; 8.5
From Leiria Castle
Donated by Francisco Hipólito Raposo,
1992, inv. 3901 to 3904

26
Loseta and *alfardon*. Manises, mid-15th
century.
Of this assemblage the *loseta* and one
alfardon are originals
10 x 18; 10 x 10
From the former Palace of the Infant
Princes, Beja
Inv. 18.3

25

26

27
Rajola. Manises?, last quarter of the 15th
century
15 x 15
From the former Palace of Alcáçova,
Lisbon
Inv. 2

27

28

28
Armillary sphere. Seville, Martinez Qui-
jarro workshop, 1508-09
14 x 14
From the Town Palace, Sintra
Inv. 19

29
National Palace, Sintra
Arab Room, early 16th-century *azulejo*
revetment

30
Pattern-tiles. Seville, F. Niculoso?,
1509-15
71 x 182
From the former Convent of Conceição,
Beja
Inv. 65

29

30

31

32 33

31
Pattern-tiles, Seville, early 16th century
27 x 27
Inv. 101

32
Azulejo. Seville, 15th-16th centuries
National Archaeological Museum
Collection
Inv. 1326

33
Azulejo panel. Seville, 16th century,1st half
23 x 23
Inv. 29

34
Azulejo panel. Seville, mid-16th century
54 x 40
Inv. 109

35
Azulejo Panel. Seville, 1508?
30 x 71
From the National Palace, Sintra, inv.
1550

34

36
Surround tile. Seville, 16th century, 1st
half
13.5 x 13.5
Acquired 1987, inv. 401

37
Ceiling plaques. Seville, 16th century,
1st half
29 x 29
Inv. 511

36

37

38
Coat-of-arms of Dom Jaime de Braganza.
Seville, c.1510
41.5 x 29
From the Ducal Palace, Vila Viçosa
Inv. 50

38

39

39
Coat-of-arms of the Dukes of Braganza
(section of ashlar). Antwerp, 1558
27 x 54
From the Ducal Palace, Vila Viçosa
Inv. 51

40
Section of ashlar with bellicose motifs.
Antwerp, 1558
54 x 54
From the Ducal Palace, Vila Viçosa
Inv. 849

40

41

42

41
Susannah and the Elders. Bacalhoa
Palace, Azeitão
Azulejo panel dating from 1565

42
Azulejo revetment, Francisco de Matos,
1584, S Roque Church,
Lisbon

43
Retable of *Our Lady of Life.* Lisbon.
Marçal de Matos, *c.*1580
500 x 465
From the former St Andrew's Church,
Lisbon

43

44

45

46

44
Retable of Our Lady of Life, St Luke

45
Retable of Our Lady of Life, Adoration
of the Shepherds

46
Retable of Our Lady of Life, the Annunciation

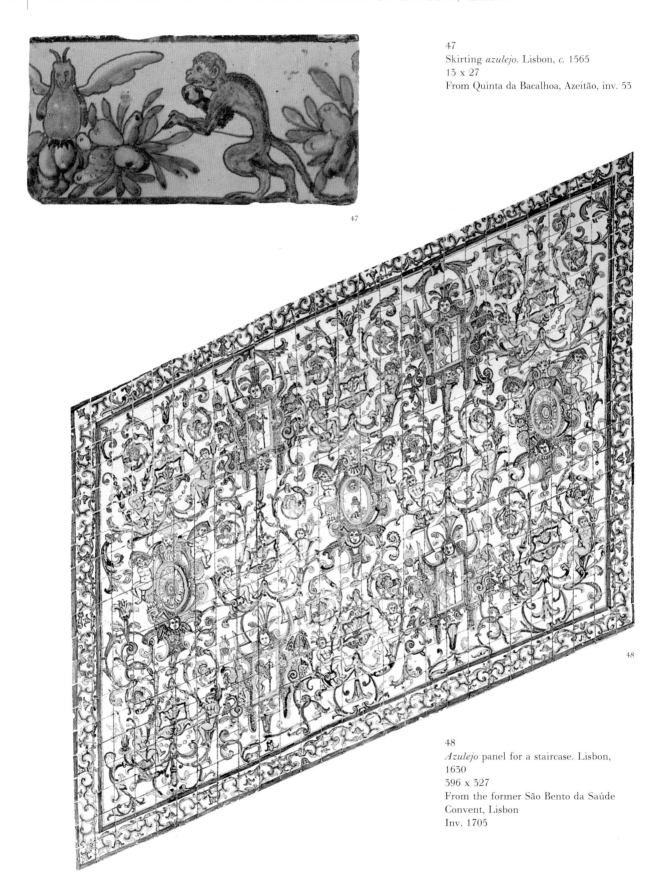

47
Skirting *azulejo*. Lisbon, *c.* 1565
13 x 27
From Quinta da Bacalhoa, Azeitão, inv. 53

47

48

48
Azulejo panel for a staircase. Lisbon, 1630
396 x 327
From the former São Bento da Saúde Convent, Lisbon
Inv. 1705

49

49
Ashlar bearing the arms of the Viscount
of Vila Nova de Cerveira. Lisbon, 1635
94 x 223
From the former Rua dos Corvos Palace,
Lisbon
Inv. 263

50

50
Ashlar with a basket of flowers on a car-
tel. Lisbon, 17th century
161 x 346
From the former Convent of Santa Clare,
Évora
Inv. 399

51
Chequered *azulejos*, Lisbon,
17th century, 1st half
79 x 110
From the Municipal Library, Oporto
Inv. 114

52
Pattern-tiles. Lisbon, 1565
67.5 x 40
From the Quinta da Bacalhoa, Azeitão
Inv. 55

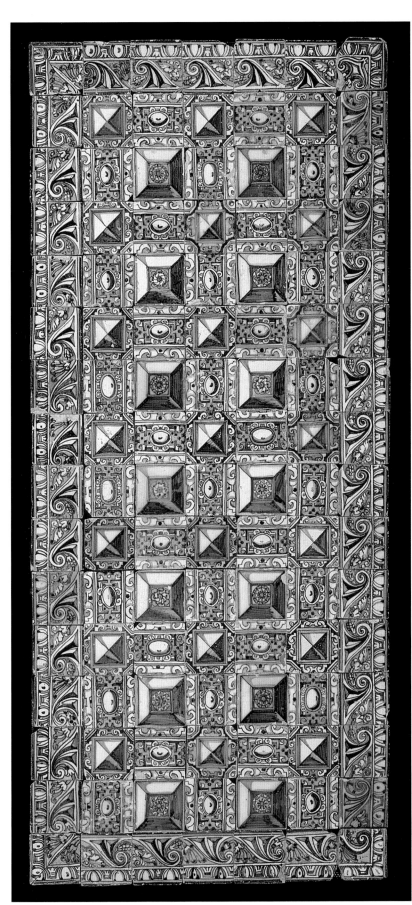

54

53
'Diamond-tipped' pattern-tile panel.
Lisbon, 17th century, 1st quarter
300 x 96
Inv. 508

54
Pattern-tile panel. Talavera de la Reina
or Lisbon?, c.1600
148.5 x 122
Acquired 1988. Inv. 909

55
Pattern-tile panel. Lisbon, 17th century,
1st quarter
170 x 110
Inv. 855

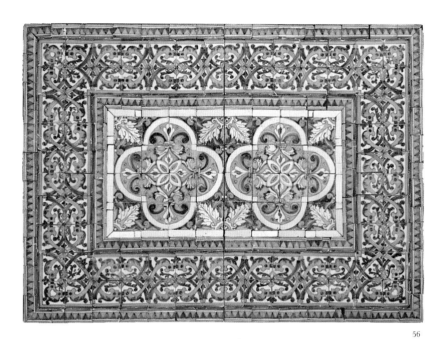

57

56

56
Pattern-tile panel. Oporto?,
mid-17th century
203 x 147
Inv. 174

57
'Camellia' pattern-tile panel. Lisbon,
1640-50
173 x 114
From the former Convent of Nossa
Senhora da Esperança, Lisbon
Inv. 147

58
Refectory of the former St Joan Convent,
now the Aveiro Museum. Integrated wall
tiling with pattern-tiles from the 1st half
of the 17th century

58

59

60

61

59
Pattern-tile panel. Lisbon, mid 17th
century
240 x 141.5; 89 x 89
Inv. 3097, 1000

60
Devotional panel, *St James*. Lisbon, mid-
17th century
84 x 70
From the Casa Pia, Lisbon
Inv. 140

61
Devotional panel, *St John the Evangelist*.
Lisbon, mid-17th century
43 x 43
From the former Convent of the Albertas,
Lisbon
Inv. 270

62
Devotional panel, *Holy Family*. Lisbon,
17th century. 1st half
43 x 45
From the former Convent of the
Albertas, Lisbon
Inv. 272

62

64

63
Albarrada. Lisbon, *c.*1680
185 x 142
From the former Convent of Nossa
Senhora da Esperança, Lisbon
National Archaeological Museum
Collection

64
Albarrada. Lisbon, *c.*1650
92 x 176
From the former Convent of Nossa
Senhora da Esperança, Lisbon
Inv. 162

65

66

65
Altar frontal. Lisbon, mid-17th century
92 x 176
From a former Carmelite Convent,
Coimbra
Machado de Castro National Museum
Collection

66
Altar frontal. Lisbon, c.1670
94 x 169.5
Inv. 388

67
Surround tile. Goa?, 17th century.
2nd quarter
10 x 20
From the St Monica Convent, Goa
Inv. 479

68
Azulejo. Goa?, 17th century. 2nd quarter
22 x 19
From the St Monica Convent, Goa
Inv. 471

67

68

69

69
The *Triumph of Amphitrite and Poseidon*. Lisbon, *c*.1670
112.5 x 279.5
From the former Odivelas Convent, Lisbon
Inv. 141

70
Satirical panel, (detail). Lisbon, *c*.1665
148.5 x 242
From the Quinta de Santo António da Cadriceira, Torres Vedras
Inv. 400

70

71

71
Leopard hunting. Lisbon, 1650-5
150 x 189.5
From the Quinta de Santo António da
Cadriceira, Torres Vedras
Inv. 137

72
Hunting animals. Lisbon, c.1680
165 x 157
From the former Praia Palace, Belém,
Lisbon
Inv. 726

72

73

74

75

73
Fronteira Palace, Gallery of the Arts,
Lisbon
Azulejo revetment, *c.*1670

74
Portrait of *Charles II of England.*
Holland/England, *c.*1662
16 x 12
Donated by the Count of Penha Garcia,
Inv. 691

75
Portrait of *Catherine of Braganza*, Queen
of England. Holland/England, *c.*1662
16 x 12
Donated by the Count of Penha Garcia,
Inv. 690

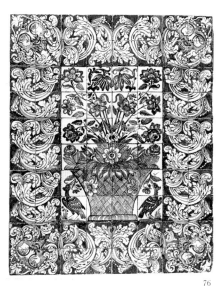

76

76
Albarrada. Lisbon, Gabriel del Barco?,
*c.*1700
141 x 111
Inv. 169

77
Great View of Lisbon, detail with
Terreiro do Paço
Lisbon, *c.*1700
Total measurements: 111.5 x 2347
From the former palace of the Counts of
Tentúgal, Lisbon
Inv. 1

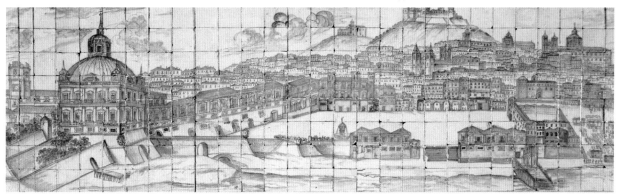

77

78

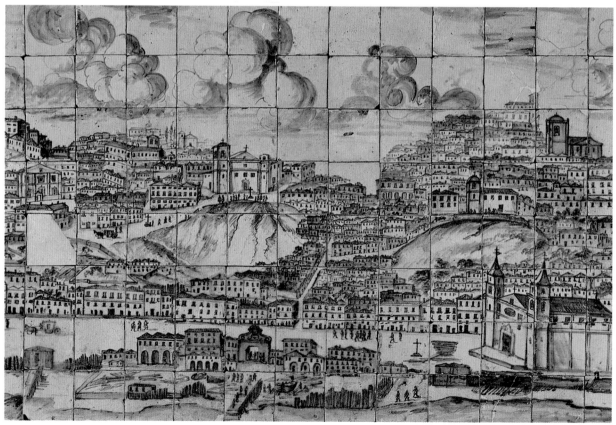

79

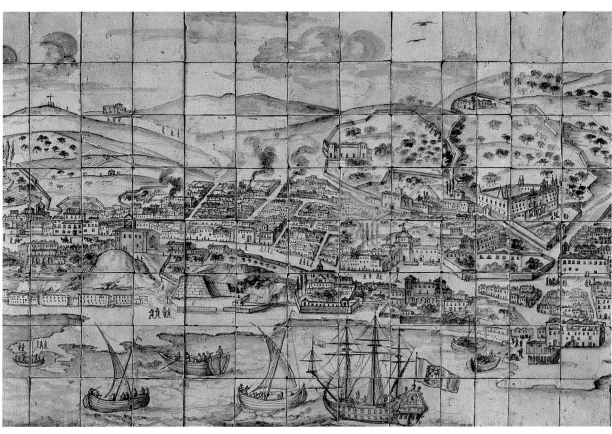

80

78
Great View of Lisbon, detail with Belém

79
Great View of Lisbon, detail with Alto de
Santa Catarina

80
Great View of Lisbon, seen from the
Olarias district

81
Dancing class. Amsterdam, Willem van
der Kloet, 1707
170 x 400
From the former Galvão Mexia Palace,
Lisbon; inv. 1680

81

82
Mythological scene. Lisbon.
Gabriel del Barco. *c.* 1695
275 x 145
Donated by José Manuel Leitão. 1972
Inv. 900

83
The *Flight into Egypt*. Lisbon.
attributed to Policarpo de Oliveira
Bernardes, *c.* 1730
57 x 99
Inv. 1690

84
Church of the Misericórdia. Evora
Wall revetment with narrative cycles
António Oliveira Bernandes, 1716

85

85
Marine scene. Lisbon, 18th century,
1st half
143 x 173
Inv. 1843

86

87

88

86
Marine and country scene. Lisbon,
18th century, 2nd quarter
199 x 440
Inv. 709

87
Alexander's Battle. Lisbon, *c.*1745
154 x 519
Inv. 680

88
Turkish Horseman. Lisbon, *c.*1745
168 x 106
Inv. 393

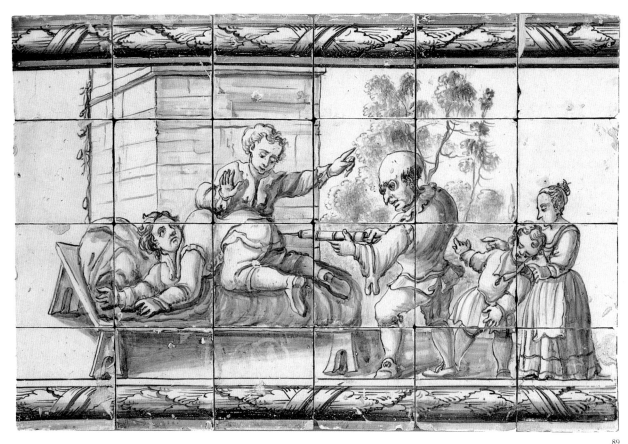

89

89
Satiric panel. Lisbon, 18th century, 1st
half
57 x 142
Donated by José Manuel Leitão, inv.
1720

90
Dutch free-standing figure tiles, c.1720,
with a Portuguese bar, c.1730
127 x 273.5
From the former Melo Palace, Lisbon
Inv. 5450

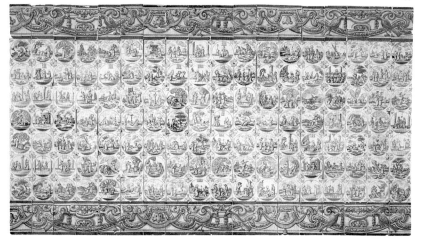

90

91

92

93

91
Free-standing figure tiles. Lisbon,
18th century, 1st half
157 x 73
Inv. 168

92
Altar frontal, 18th century
80 x 193.5
Inv. 883

93
Devotional panel, the *Archangel St
Michael.* 18th century, 1st half
70 x 56
Inv. 3221

94

94
Jesus in the Midst of the Doctors. Lisbon,
c.1760
196 x 300
From the former monastery of Santo
António da Convalescença, Lisbon
Inv. 866

95
Devotional panel, *Our Lady and St
Dominic.* Lisbon, 1771
176 x 126
Acquired 1988, inv. 1643

96
Alminha. Coimbra, 18th century,
2nd half
38.5 x 26
Acquired 1994, inv. 6178

95   96

97
Welcome figure, Lisbon, *c.*1770
200 x 71
Acquired 1994, inv. 6178

98
Detail of a large panel, *Four Seasons.*
Lisbon, 18th century, 2nd half
280 x 98
Inv. 735

99
Free-standing figure-tile. Bristol,
*c.*1760-70
13 x 13
Donated by Anthony and Veronica Ray
in memory of João Miguel dos Santos
Simões, 1972, inv. 412

100
Pombaline pattern-tile panel. Lisbon,
*c.*1760-80
98 x 112
Inv. 914

99

100

101
Didactic plaque. Coimbra, 18th century,
2nd half
20 x 20
Donated by architect Carlos Sanchez
Jorge, 1989, inv. c-14

101

102

102
Gardens of the Palace de Queluz.
Detail of the wall revetment of the
canal. 1755

103
Ashlar with eagles and dolphins. Lisbon,
late 18th century
98 x 264
From the former palace of the Marquis
of Nisa
Inv. 226

104
Ashlar with eagle and dolphin (detail).
Lisbon, late 18th century
98 x 264
From the former palace of the Marquis
of Nisa
Inv. 226

103

105

105-110
The Story of António Joaquim Carneiro,
hatter. Lisbon, Real Fábrica do Rato,
*c.*1800
83 x 118 (each)
From the Quinta do Chapeleiro, Póvoa
de Santo Adrião
Inv. 227a,c,d,e,f,g

106

107

108

109

110

111
Pattern-tiles for façades. Lisbon, 19th
century, 2nd half
87.5 x 54.5
Acquired 1995, inv. 5967

112
Pattern-tiles for façades. Oporto, Fábrica
de Massarelos, 19th century, 2nd half
147.5 x 121.5
Donated by the World's President
Organization, 1993, inv. 5905

111

112

113

113
Façade of a building in Largo Rafael
Bordalo Pinheiro, Lisbon, 1864

114
Flowered vase. Lisbon, Luís António
Ferreira (1807-?), *c.*1860
135 x 81
Donated by architect José Lico, 1994,
inv. 5930

115
Columns bearing masonic inscriptions.
Lisbon, Luís António Ferreira *c.*1860
124.5 x 41.5
Acquired 1988, inv. 1789 to 1792

114

116
Battle of Ourique. Carlos Lopes Pavilion,
Lisbon, panel by Jorge Colaço,
1922/1927

115

OURIQUE

117
The arrival of St Auta's relics at the
Madre de Deus Church
Lisbon, Pereira Cão, late 19th century

117

118

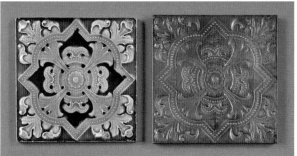

119

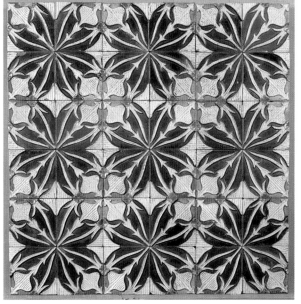

120

118
Façade in Rua dos Anjos, Lisbon, with tiles in semi-relief, 20th century, 1st half

119
Relief tile and die. Lisbon, Fábrica de Louça de Sacavém, early 20th century
16 x 16
Donated by Clive Gilbert, 1992, inv. 4147; T-2

120
Pattern-tiles. Caldas da Rainha, Fábrica de Faianças das Caldas da Rainha, late 19th century
78 x 78
From Rua da Graça, 178, Lisbon
Inv. 187

121
Portrait of *King Manuel II*. Lisbon,
Fábrica de Louça de Sacavém, 1908
16 x 15.5
Donated by Clive Gilbert, 1992,
inv. 4146

122
João Costa, Ceramic plaque. Lisbon, 1885
31 x 12
Acquired 1990, inv. C-46

121

123
Azulejo panel, detail. France,
Sarreguemines Factory, late 19th century
137 x 191
Inv. 1632

122

123

124

124
Azulejo panel. Lisbon, *c.* 1920
400 x 276
From the Padaria Independente, Lisbon
Inv. 239

125

125
Rafael Bordalo Pinheiro. Plaque, 1905
18 x 18
Acquired 1989, inv. C-8

126
Rafael Bordalo Pinheiro (1846-1905),
Pattern-tiles, early 20th century
88 x 55
Inv. 185

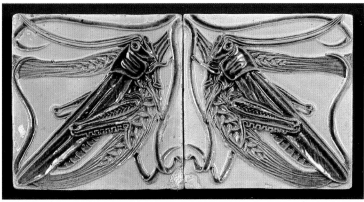

126

127

127
Tile. Bonn, Wessel Factory, c.1900
15 x 15
Anonymous gift, 1992, inv. 4610

128
Free-standing figure and border tiles.
England, c.1900
16 x 16; 15 x 7.5
Inv. 460, 463, 464, 468

128

129

129
Pattern-tiles. Lisbon, Fábrica de Louça
de Sacavém, c.1910
48 x 48
Acquired, 1990, inv. 3113

130
Pattern-tiles for façades. Lisbon, Fábrica
de Louça de Sacavém, c.1910
200 x 47
Acquired 1993, inv. 5894

131
Alfredo Pinto. Façade decoration project,
1911
33 x 32
Inv. P-1

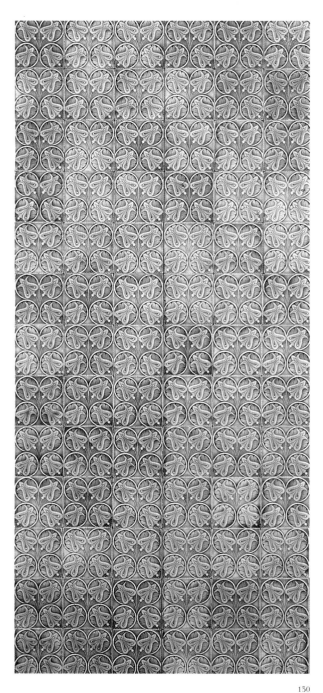

130

131

132
Raul Lino. Pattern-tile panel, 1915
84 x 84
Inv. 175

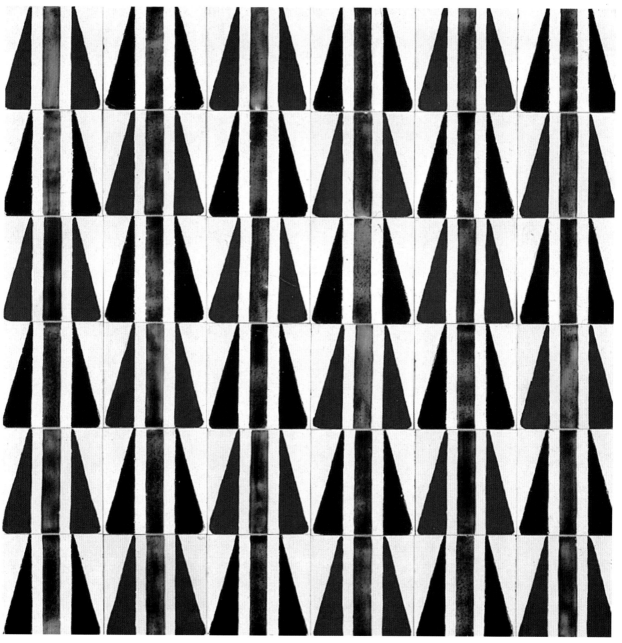

133

134

133
Raul Lino. Pattern-tile panel, 1970
based on a project of *c*.1910
68 x 39
Inv. 3129

134
Pattern-tile panel. Lisbon, Fábrica de
Louça de Sacavém, 1930-40
94 x 62.5
Acquired 1992, inv. 3244

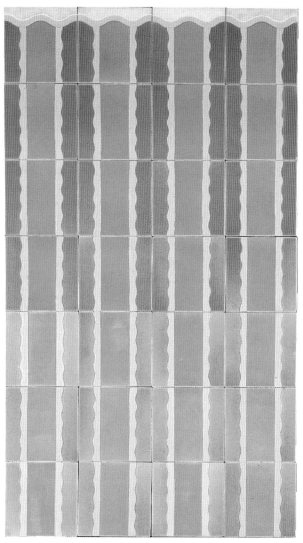

135
Pattern-tile panel. Lisbon, Fábrica
Lusitânia, *c.*1930
105 x 60
Acquired by the Museum, 1990, inv.
1725

136
Lambrilha (miniature tile) panel,
1937-42. Projects by Paulo Ferreira,
Tom and F. Kradolfer
52 x 122.5
Inv. 1934

135

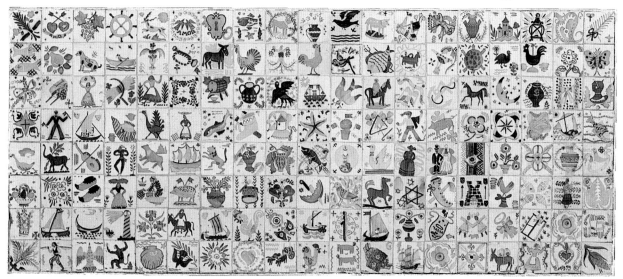

136

137

137
Jorge Barradas. Pattern-tile panel,
c. 1950
84.5 x 70
Inv. 183

138
Maria Keil. Wall panel for Socorro
Station, 1966
168 x 70
Donated by the Lisbon Metropolitano,
1989, inv. 1650

139
Maria Keil. Panel for Rossio Station,
1963
168 x 70
Donated by the Lisbon Metropolitano,
1989, inv. 1628

138

140

140
Sá Nogueira (b. 1921).
Panel for Laranjeiras Station, 1988
197 x 99
Donated by the Lisbon Metropolitano,
1990, inv. 2020

141
Manuel Cargaleiro (b.1927).
Azulejo panel, 1985
98 x 98
Donated by the artist, 1985, inv. 246

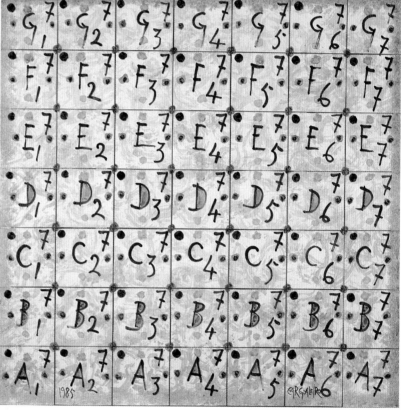

141

142
Manuel Cargaleiro
Panel for Colégio Militar Station, 1987
197 x 84
Donated by the Lisbon Metropolitano,
1990, inv. 1936

1988

CARGALEIRO

142

143
Artur José. *Geometries, c.*1985
112 x 56
Donated by the artist, 1993, inv. 5927

144
Eduardo Nery. *Vibration II*, 1987
100 x 150
Donated by the artist, 1987, inv. 364

145
João Abel Manta. *Azulejo* panel, 1972
100 x 170
Donated by the artist, 1991, inv. 3117

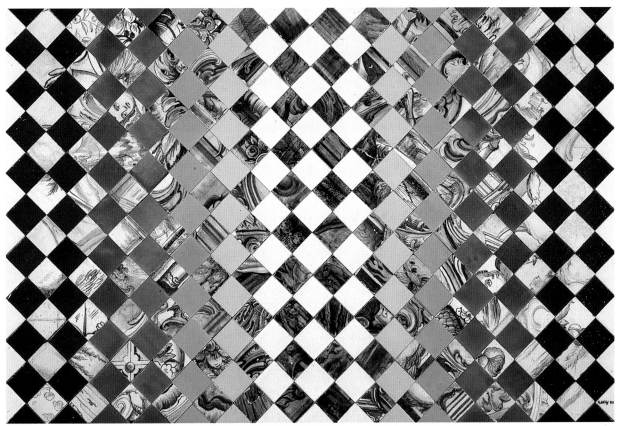

144

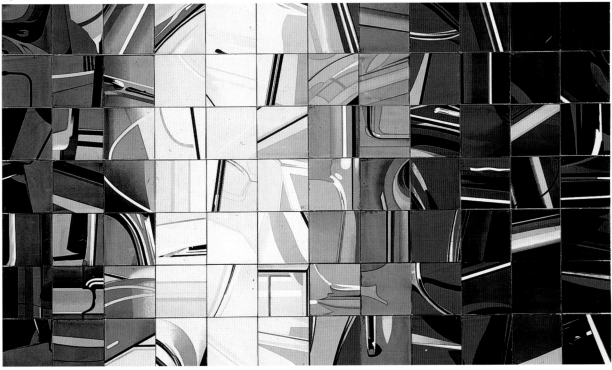

145

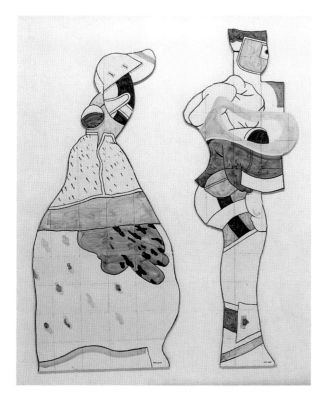

147

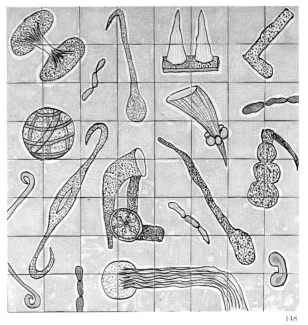

148

149

146
Querubim Lapa (b. 1925). Chequered-
azulejo panel, 1991
68 x 131
Donated by the artist, 1994, inv. 5977

147
Luís Pinto Coelho. Welcome figures.
1980
153 x 78; 167 x 56
Donated by the artist, 1980, inv. 1630,
1631

148
Arnold Zimmerman. Untitled, 1991
116 x 115
Donated by the artist and by Cerâmicas
Ratton, 1992, inv. 5929

149
Maria Helena Vieira da Silva. Free-
standing figures, 1987
28 x 28
Donated by the artist, 1987, inv. 356
to 259

150

151

150
Urn. Real Fábrica do Rato, Tomás
Brunetto period (1767-71)
70 x 50 x 50
National Museum of Ancient Art

151
Wenceslau Cifka. Amphora, 1877
39.6 x 22 x 25
Acquired 1984, inv. C-42

152
Rafael Bordalo Pinheiro. Table
centrepiece, 1896
38 x 55 x 38
Museum of Chiado

152

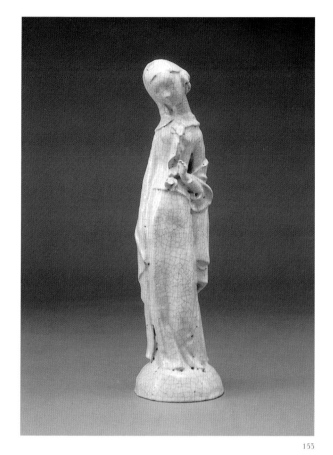

153

154

153
Jorge Barradas (1894-1971). Female
figure, mid-20th century (c.1950)
40 x 8 x 8
Acquired 1988, inv. C-10

154
Hein Semke (1899–1995). Plaque, 1962
37.5 x 37.5
Acquired 1987, inv. C-6

155
Querubim Lapa (b. 1925). Decorative
plaque, 1987
37 x 51
Donated by the artist, 1994, inv. C-89

155

156
Maria João Oliveira. *Tribute
to Tàpies*, 1987
42 x 58
Donated by the artist, 1994,
inv. C-92

157
Suzana Barros, *Moulding*
30 x 55 x 55
Donated by the artist, 1991,
Inv. C-65

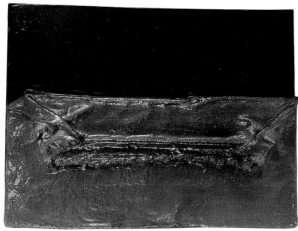

156

157

158

158
Cecília de Sousa (b. 1937). *Diptych*, 1989
62 x 62
Donated by Ensul, 1991, inv. C-67

GLOSSARY

AEROGRAPHY (technique): Direct application of paint on the body by means of an aerograph (air-brush), using zinc stencils.

ALBARRADA: Flower vase flanked by two birds, in existence since the 2nd half of the 17th century. In the 18th century repetition of the motif formed panels in series.

ALFARDON: Hexagonal flooring-tile, laid around a *loseta*, forming octagonal patterns. Produced in Valencia in the 15th and 1st half of the 16th century (see *Loseta*).

ALMINHA: An individual tile or small panel representing souls in purgatory involved in flames. At the bottom P.N.–A.M. (Our Father – Ave Maria).

ASHLAR *silhar:* A tile lining of variable height, placed from floor level to part way up the wall.

AZULEJO: Ceramic plaque of varying size and thickness, consisting of a clay body and a decorated and glazed surface.

BISCUIT OR BODY: Clay fired once, ready to be coated with *engobe*, enamel, or glaze and fired anew: hence the term 'biscotto' (twice fired).

'CARPET' *tapete*: Lining of repetitive patterns on large wall surfaces.

CARTEL: 'Cartouche', a frame made from folio motifs.

CHEQUERED *AZULEJO: enxaque-tado*: An assemblage, arranged to be read diagonally, of tiles of variable geometric shapes and sizes, separated by rectangular strips and/or borders. Used in revetments from the 2nd half of the 16th century to the middle of the 17th century.

COURRONEMENT: A wheel-window in Gothic architecture.

CUENCA azulejo de aresta (technique): Application of wood or metal moulds to the raw clay, forming raised edges that separate the various coloured enamels. This technique appeared in Seville towards the end of the 15th century and was used throughout the 16th century in place of the *cuerda seca* technique (*see Cuerda seca*).

CUERDA SECA corda seca (technique): Outlining decorative motifs with grooves filled with a mixture of fat (linseed oil) and manganese. This prevents the colours running together during the second firing (*see Cuenca*).

DEVOTIONAL PANEL *registo*: A devotional panel placed on building façades, invoking the protection of the Virgin or the Saints against cataclysms.

ENAMELLING *esmaltagem* (technique)*:* Covering the tile with a transparent or opaque vitreous substance that solidifies after melting, providing impermeability and gloss.

ENGOBE: Very fine liquid clay applied to the tile body as a decoration prior to firing.

FAÇADE *AZULEJO azulejo de fachada*: Patterned, or sometimes figurative, tiles used in building revetments, widespread from the 2nd quarter of the 19th century.

FAIENCE: See *Majolica*

FERRONERIE *cartouches*: An ornamental motif of decorative scrolled patterns of Flemish origin. Used in the 2nd half of the 16th century.

FRAME *guarnição:* Borders an assemblage by means of a single row of tiles (surrounds and friezes) or of double rows (bars).

FREE-STANDING FIGURE TILE *azulejo de figura avulsa:* Contains on a single tile the principal motif — flowers, fruit, animals, human figures, boats, baskets, varied constructions — generally with a decoration at each corner.

INDUSTRIAL TILE *azulejo industrial:* Production-line tiles decorated by mechanical means, for façades and shop interiors and the entrance halls of residential buildings. It appeared in the mid-19th century.

LAMBRILHA: A small *azulejo*, painted, stencilled or stamped.

LEAD-GLAZING *vidrado plumbífero:* Transparent glaze resulting from the addition of lead oxide, which completely coats the tile.

LOSETA: A square tile used in assemblages with *alfardons* or plain terracotta tiles (see *Alfardon*).

LUSTRE *reflexo metálico:* Decoration obtained by firing twice. The first firing, using a high-temperature kiln, fixes the tin glazing; the second, at a low temperature, gives rise to the deposition of oxides of silver, copper or iron which provide a metallic sheen.

MAJOLICA or FAIENCE (technique): Coating with tin-glaze following the first firing, after which painting was applied by brush. Used in Portugal since the middle of the 16th century. The noun is an Italian word for tin-glazed earthenware and is properly used in English for Italian wares and those made in imitation.

MECHANICAL STAMPING *estampagem mecânica* (technique): Printing a design by means of dots on the glaze, in a single colour. Later than stencilling.

MUDÉJAR: Decorative system based on Moorish art, in vogue in the Iberian Peninsula in the 15th and 16th centuries.

PATTERN *padrão:* Geometric or floral composition of a variable number of tiles (see 'Carpet').

RAJOLAS: Square flooring plaques, decorated in blue and purple over tin glazing. Produced in Valencia in the 15th century and first half of the 16th.

RELIEF *relevo* (technique): Marking designs on tile blanks by means of the concave outline of wood or metal stamps.

SGRAFFITO esgrafitado (technique): Scratching through the top surface of two layers, outlining the decorative motif and revealing the colour of the bottom layer.

STENCILLING *estampilhagem* (technique): Painting by brush through cut-outs in waxed paper applied over the glazing of the tile.

TILE-MOSAICS *alicatados:* Combinations of fragments of glazed ceramics of many colours and geometric shapes, cut out prior to firing.

TIN-GLAZE *vidrado estanífero:* White, opaque glaze resulting from the addition of tin oxide. Used to coat one surface of a tile.

TRIPOD *trempe:* Small tripod of refractory material placed between the tiles during firing.

WELCOME FIGURE *figura de convite:* A life-size figure of a lackey, halberdier, lady or warrior, in a pose of welcome, placed in entrance halls, on staircases and in gardens. Not to be confused with figurative or patterned wainscoting.

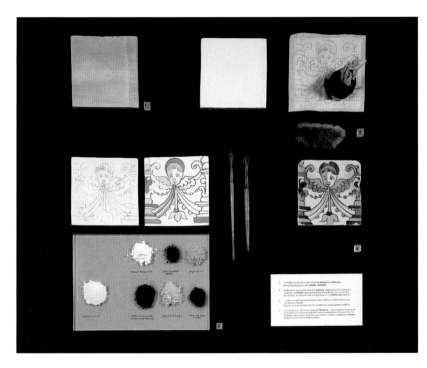

159
Majolica technique (Educational display case)

BIBLIOGRAPHY

MADRE DE DEUS CONVENT

Belém, Frey Jerónimo de. *Crónica Seráfica da Santa Província dos Algarves de Regular Observância do ... Padre S. Francisco*, vol. 3, 1750-5

Lacerda, Aarão de. *A Madre de Deus*, Barcelos, Portucalense Editora, 1940

Raczynski, A.. *Les Arts au Portugal*, Paris, 1847

Sabugosa, Conde de. *A Rainha D. Leonor 1458-1525*, Lisbon, Ed. Império, 1921

Santa Maria, Frey Agostinho de. *Santuário Mariano*, vol. 1, Lisbon, Ant. Pedroso Galram Workshop, 1707

Telles, Liberato. *Duas palavras sobre pavimentos*, Lisbon, 1896

Telles, Liberato. *Mosteiro e Igreja da Madre de Deus*, Lisbon, Imprensa Nacional, 1899

AZULEJO

Azulejo (journal), nºs 1 & 2, Lisbon, Museu Nacional do Azulejo

Brussels, 1991. *Azulejo* (catalogue), Európália 91 – Portugal, 1991

Calado, Rafael Salinas. *Azulejo: 5 séculos de azulejo em Portugal*, Lisbon, ed. Correios e Telecomunicações de Portugal, 1986

Correia, Virgílio. *Azulejos*, Coimbra, 1956

Lisbon, 1947. *Azulejos* (catalogue), Museu Nacional do Azulejo, 1947

Lisbon, 1989. Maria Keil – *Azulejos* (catalogue), Museu Nacional do Azulejo, 1989

Lisbon, 1994. *Querubim: obra cerâmica 1954-1994* (catalogue), Museu Nacional do Azulejo, 1994

Lisbon 94. *Influência oriental na cerâmica portuguesa do século XVII* (catalogue), Museu Nacional do Azulejo, 1994

Meco, José. *Azulejaria Portuguesa*, Lisbon, Bertrand Editora, 1985

Meco, José. *O Azulejo em Portugal*, Lisbon, Publicações Alfa, 1989

Paris, 1994. *Azulejos: Les Métamorphoses de l'Azur* (catalogue), Paris, Espace Electra, 1994

Pereira, João Castel-Branco. *Azulejos no Metropolitano de Lisboa*, Metropolitano de Lisboa, 1990

Queirós, José. *Cerâmica Portuguesa*, 2nd edition, enlarged, 1948

Queirós, José, *Cerâmica portuguesa e outros estudos*, Lisbon, 1987

Santos, Reynaldo dos. *O Azulejo em Portugal*, Lisbon, 1957

Saporiti, Teresa. *Azulejos de Lisboa do século XX*, Lisbon, Edições Afrontamento, 1992

Simões, J.M. dos Santos. *Os azulejos do Paço de Vila Viçosa*, Lisbon, 1946

Simões, J.M. dos Santos. *Carreaux céramiques hollandais au Portugal et en Espagne*, The Hague, 1959

Simões, J.M. dos Santos. *Azulejaria em Portugal nos Açores e na Madeira*, Lisbon, Calouste Gulbenkian Foundation, 1963

Simões, J.M. dos Santos. *Azulejaria portuguesa no Brasil 1500-1882*, Lisbon, Calouste Gulbenkian Foundation, 1965

Simões, J.M. dos Santos. *Azulejaria em Portugal nos séculos XV e XVI*, Lisbon, Calouste Gulbenkian Foundation, 1969

Simões, J.M. dos Santos. *Azulejaria em Portugal no século XVII*, 2 vols. Lisbon, Calouste Gulbenkian Foundation, 1971

Simões, J.M. dos Santos. *Azulejaria em Portugal no século XVIII*, Lisbon, Calouste Gulbenkian Foundation, 1979

Smith, Robert C.. *The Art of Portugal 1500-1800*, London, New York, George Weidenfeld and Nicolson, 1968

Veloso, Barros; Almasqué, Isabel. *Azulejos de Fachada em Lisboa*, Lisbon City Council, 1989

160
Panel painted by children of the primary school no. 151, Lisbon, 1990

INDEX